SOUL PURPOSE

SOUL PURPOSE

J.John

Authentic

MILTON KEYNES ● COLORADO SPRINGS ● HYDERABAD

14 13 12 11 10 09 08   7 6 5 4 3 2 1

First published 2008 by Authentic Media
9 Holdom Avenue, Bletchley, Milton Keynes, Bucks, MK1 1QR, UK
1820 Jet Stream Drive, Colorado Springs, CO 80921, USA
OM Authentic Media, Medchal Road, Jeedimetla Village,
Secunderabad 500 055, A.P., India
www.authenticmedia.co.uk

*Authentic Media is a division of IBS-STL U.K., limited by guarantee, with
its Registered Office at Kingstown Broadway, Carlisle,
Cumbria, CA3 0HA. Registered in England & Wales No. 1216232.
Registered charity 270162*

British Library Cataloguing in Publication Data

A catalogue record for this book is available from the
British Library

ISBN-13: 978-1-86024-624-5

Cover Design by Chris Jones
Print Management by Adare
Printed in the UK by CPI Bookmarque, Croydon, CR0 4TD

Contents

Foreword

Being a Christian has never been easy and right now is perhaps one of the most difficult times. This is not because of persecution or opposition, but simply because the essence of Christianity seems to have got lost for so many people in the supposedly Christian culture we have developed over the centuries. What's this religion about? Who was Jesus? Can he really be relevant for me today? Is a life transformation actually possible?

This book will help you reconnect with the real message of the New Testament. It will help you discover – or rediscover – what the gospel can mean for you in your very own life, whatever your situation, whatever your hopes, whatever your qualifications, whatever your past. My good friend J.John is always prepared to reveal his own weaknesses in the interests of helping other people come to a better understanding. He does not set himself up on some pedestal so that we can all admire him. He is a human just like you and me and – as you will see as you read further – he is willing to grapple with, and search for, answers to many of the problems that new Christians face. This is not surprising really when you consider just how many people he has inspired to follow Jesus. Travelling around from country to country, he has spoken to literally thousands of people over the last thirty years. What fascinates me most about him is not that he has got this amazing ability to help people through his own honesty and conviction, but that he has also seen healings occur – while he has been talking – because he has inspired that much faith in God. It is good to hear about a few biblical miracles being brought into the current day.

Perhaps you personally don't need a miracle to help you believe. Perhaps you just need to come to a better understanding of what this whole Christianity thing is all about. Perhaps you just need to work out how believing in Jesus can have a real effect on your life. Perhaps you just need a bit more food for thought. Perhaps you want to work out how your sole purpose in life can become your *soul purpose*. Enjoy reading, but please don't stop there. Use this little manual to kick-start your life. If you are already a Christian and you are reading out of interest, why not take up the challenge of thinking just how much you are acting on all that J.John writes about? Let his truthful words sink deep into your heart so that you can move on to better and bigger things and a much brighter future. And remember, however daunting the Christian path might seem, God's on your side. What can you possibly fear?

Happy reading!

Mike Pilavachi, Soul Survivor

Introduction

What does it mean to be a follower of Jesus in the twenty-first century?

Our world bombards us with a forceful message: we must strive to live independent lives, and we must do it on our own and for ourselves. The concept of holistic, unadulterated dependence on another person is almost offensive within our culture. But if you believe that the message of Jesus is true, you are called to be his disciple, a follower committed to a lifelong journey of total dependence: loving him, leaning on him and learning from him. It would be a great mistake to underestimate the significance of becoming a disciple of Jesus Christ – the word 'disciple' occurs no less than 290 times in the New Testament.

We learn in Matthew 28:19,20 (NIV) that the task of a disciple is to make other disciples and to teach them to follow Jesus' ways. Jesus said: 'Go and make disciples of all nations, baptising them in the name of the Father and of the Son and of the Holy Spirit, and teaching them to obey everything I have commanded you. And surely I am with you always, to the very end of the age.' Before you can start making disciples and before you can teach people how to follow Jesus, you need to understand more yourself.

If you are new to Christianity or have recently returned to your faith in Jesus, you are setting out on the most difficult but worthwhile journey of your life. This book will equip you with the essentials you need to travel that journey with strength, passion and endurance, whatever the bumps and potholes on your way. May it bless and encourage you.

J.John

1

The Message

The tipping point in my own encounter with Christ came when I read Revelation 3:20: 'Look! I stand at the door and knock. If you hear my voice and open the door, I will come in, and we will share a meal together as friends.' On 9 February 1975, I realised that Jesus loved me and I decided to invite him into my life. It was only later that I fully understood the message that he brought when he lived on this earth so many years ago. Have you asked Jesus into your life? Are you wondering how well you understand the message that he brought to us?

Misunderstanding

I spend much of my time travelling and speaking with people from different countries and cultures. Over the years, I've found that many people's understanding of the message of Christianity is in fact a misunderstanding. Sadly, I've even seen churches misrepresenting the message. For example, I once saw a poster outside a church that merely said:

'Have a nice day!' That was hardly the message of the early church – you don't throw someone wishing you 'a nice day' to the lions! Even if we don't go as far in watering things down as that, there is always a temptation in our politically correct society to remove the unpopular elements from the Christian message.

Many people misunderstand Christianity because of their preconceptions. So when someone asks me what I do for a living, I don't always give an obvious answer. Once I was sitting on a plane and when the woman in the adjacent seat asked about my job I told her, 'I'm a motivational speaker for behavioural alteration.' My motive in giving unusual answers is to challenge people to consider the message of Christianity from a fresh perspective.

When you or I approach any new idea we come at it with a cluster of our own opinions. Our past experiences are part of who we are and they matter. But as you read this book, I challenge you to try to gently remove the labels that you have stuck on Christianity. Come on a short journey with me and explore what the Christian message is really all about.

The Good News

The Greek word 'gospel' means 'Good News'. Can we still consider the message of the New Testament Good News today?

The Good News

The Greek word 'gospel' means 'Good News'. Can we still consider the message of the New Testament Good News today?

How Would You Feel?

Imagine you suddenly pass out of this life and wake up sitting alone in a large, empty cinema. The screen looms before you. Suddenly, an angel flies in, stops next to you and says, 'Welcome to the cinema of judgement. Relax, just watch the screen.' Then you watch the film of your life – everything you ever did, said or thought. At the end, the angel says, 'Relax. There is going to be a second showing. All the people featured in the film are queuing outside and now we are going to let them in to enjoy it, too.'

How would you feel if your life was judged on that basis? Actually, that is exactly how God does judge us: by everything we have thought, said and done. And we are not only judged by the sins we have committed, we are also judged by what we omitted to do. The apostle James (one of Jesus' own brothers, who was also a leader of the Jerusalem church) says, 'Remember, it is sin to know what you ought to do and then not do it' (James 4:17).

Often, we go through life presuming we haven't done anything wrong, until we really stop to think about it. A man once went to court, pleading his innocence. He listened for several hours to the court proceedings, and then shouted: 'I'm guilty!' The judge turned to him and said, 'Why didn't you say that several hours ago?'

> *Often, we go through life presuming we haven't done anything wrong, until we really stop to think about it.*

'Well,' replied the man, 'I didn't realise I was guilty, until I'd heard all the evidence!'

Many times I have done things I should not have – and I have failed to do things that would have been right at the time. There have been occasions when I could have been kind, but I chose not to. There have been moments when I could have been generous, but wasn't. When I dwell on my mistakes, I often feel overwhelmed by the task of trying to somehow improve myself. I know that in my own strength I haven't got what it takes to become a less selfish person.

Our culture is obsessed with DIY. It is not just home improvements that we are into, though; rather it is the desire to improve the self that gets so many people up in the morning. Many of us give almost, if not all of, our time trying to improve our jobs, enhance our looks, enlarge our bank accounts and upgrade our belongings – or aspiring to do so! National spending is a good indicator of this reality: currently we spend around £10.5 billion annually on grooming products, and market research company Mintel have estimated that by 2009 UK residents will be spending £11 million on house wares and £912 million on plastic surgery. But deep down, do we really expect that having a new car, wardrobe, better body, modern home or better bank balance will actually transform us?

Only Jesus offers us a real and lasting life trans-formation that is truly satisfying. Only he is the fulfilment of the hope that we often channel into our search for one or many of these material things.

I do not wish to flatly condemn all these things as wrong – some of them may take right, honourable places in our lives. But since the beginning of time, humankind has looked for satisfaction, meaning and completion outside of God – leading us to a confused, godless version of living. Only Jesus offers us true life in all fullness. That is why the message that he brought is still astonishingly Good News today.

The Catch

There is a catch, though. If we want a fantastic transformation to take place in our lives, we need to believe in Jesus, repent and resolve to follow Jesus from now on. Let's take a closer look at each of these aspects to developing a relationship with God.

Believing in Jesus

Jesus commands us to put aside our doubts and believe in God and in him. The Algerian Christian known as St Augustine, who lived AD 354–430 and is considered one of the fathers of the Western church, said, 'Faith is to believe what you do not see; the reward of this faith is to see what you believe.' Faith is believing what God says, simply because it was God who said it. Sounds a bit risky? It is. But it is only in taking the risk of believing that we allow ourselves the opportunity to experience the reward of 'seeing what we believe'.

In the movie *Indiana Jones and the Last Crusade* there is a scene when Indiana must step out onto an invisible bridge that crosses an enormous cavern.

> *As he steps out in courage and faith, the bridge rises to form beneath his feet, creating his passage to safety.*

As he steps out in courage and faith, the bridge rises to form beneath his feet, creating his passage to safety. Logic tells us to ask for some evidence before we believe something to be true or correct, hence many people want a sign to prove God's existence (and goodness) before they take the step of believing in him. When Jesus walked on the earth as a human being, many people believed he was the Messiah (the one sent from God) because of the miracles he performed. '"After all," they said, "would you expect the Messiah to do more miraculous signs than this man has done?"' (John 7:31). However, it is recorded that others weren't affected by these wonders: 'But despite all the miraculous signs Jesus had done, most of the people still did not believe in him' (John 12:37).

Jesus himself rebuked people who demanded miracles as a condition for their belief: 'Will you never believe in me unless you see miraculous signs and wonders?' he asked (John 4:48). So miracles, it seems, are not to be considered signs for triggering belief, instead they are the fruit of faith. In Mark 16:17, we are told that miraculous signs will accompany those who believe. Taking the apparently irrational leap of faith in God might seem illogical – but when you do so, you will start to see signs of God all around you. Perhaps the most convincing one will be that of your own personal transformation.

Who is this Jesus?

The historical evidence for the existence of Jesus in AD 33 is extremely convincing – in fact we have more evidence that a real historical figure called Jesus existed than we do for Julius Caesar! But who was Jesus, and what was his message? Take a closer look with me at the society that Jesus came into . . .

> *Like many people today, most people 2,000 years ago had turned away from God and were ignoring or denying his existence.*

Like many people today, most people 2,000 years ago had turned away from God and were ignoring or denying his existence. Somehow, though, they still knew that their lifestyle was wrong, so they lived with a feeling of guilt and shame. Their lives were characterised by fear and whenever their true nature surfaced they tried to pass the blame onto someone else. They argued constantly, usually about whose fault it was, and they had particular problems with members of the opposite sex! Does this sound familiar?

Although the world then was a very different place to ours in terms of development, people largely thought and behaved as we do today. Their attempts at doing good or being religious were flawed. Religious practices were used to build up egos, and pride made individuals enormously intolerant of others. Instead of loving those around them, people were easily irritated and resentful. Furthermore, the fear that eventually they might face judgement for their mistakes left people dreading death. They lived for the moment, trying to blot out thoughts of any repercussions for the selfish, immoral lives they led. They had become oblivious to the suffering around them, and were desperately trying to ignore the misery inherent in society.

Society was in denial. And many people had got to the point where they preferred the misery of their present situation to the unknown prospect of change. Perhaps this was because of the well-known psychological phenomenon that occurs among long-term prisoners: the prospect of freedom can become almost terrifying. The old, destructive habits had become so familiar that they felt safe.

Imagine for a moment how God, who created a wonderful, perfect world, must have felt when he looked on that sort of society. He saw people who had lost touch with him by making sinful choices, and it hurt him. God, perfect himself, can't tolerate our sin – it puts a barrier between himself and us. Sin prevents us from enjoying the loving, personal relationship that God wants to have with us.

The Envoy

Who would be qualified to represent both sides in the breakdown in communication between God and humankind?

> *While Jesus had a human mother, he also had miraculous powers: he was able to create food and drink out of virtually nothing, he healed the sick and he even brought people back from the dead.*

This is where Jesus comes in. The mediator could only be someone who was both fully God and fully human; Jesus Christ was uniquely qualified. The Gospels speak of him as both 'Son of God' and 'Son of Man', indicating that Jesus is simultaneously perfect God and perfect man. While Jesus had a human mother, he also had miraculous powers: he was able to create food and drink out of virtually nothing, he healed the sick and he even brought people back from the dead.

You Are Infinitely Special to God

God loves every single human unconditionally. He purposefully created you and me, and when he did so he paid intricate attention to detail. He made us in the image of himself, which means that we have the potential to relate to him and become like him.

Picture a £20 note that has been crumpled and torn. Whatever state it is in, it is still worth £20. In God's eyes, you are worth a whole lot more than £20 – to him you are priceless. Regardless of your behaviour – in the past, present or future – your value can never change in God's eyes. He is love, and he created you in and for and through his love.

Rick Warren expresses the miracle of our creation and our worth to God brilliantly in *The Purpose Driven Life* (Zondervan Publishing House, 2003). He writes:

> You are not an accident. Your birth was no mistake or mishap, and your life is no fluke of nature. Your parents may not have planned you, but God did . . . Long before your parents conceived you, you were conceived in the mind of God. He thought of you first. It is not fate, nor chance, nor luck, nor coincidence that you are breathing at this moment. You are alive because God wanted to create you! The Bible says, 'The Lord will fulfil his purpose for me'.
> (Psalm 138:8a)

Humanity is worth so much to God that he cannot bear to see the people he created lost and living without him. Because of this, God sent his Son Jesus to earth in order to restore his relationship with humankind and bring us the help that we so desperately need.

Jesus Paid the Price

Imagine for a moment that you have just popped into the corner shop. You have left your car on the double-yellow line outside while you pick up a loaf of bread. You are at the till when, from the corner of your eye, you notice a traffic warden sticking a ticket on your car. You run out of the shop trying desperately to think up an excuse. Before you manage to garble anything, the warden looks at you and smiles warmly. She gets out her chequebook, and scribbles out a cheque. Then she hands it to you and slowly walks away. It covers the full amount of your fine.

That is what God did for us in sending Jesus to die for us. Although all the evidence of our thoughts, words and actions prove we are guilty of turning our backs on God, he paid the price that we owe for our mistakes: eternal separation from him. Jesus died on a cross, taking the punishment we deserve on himself, so that we can be reconciled with God. In 1 Peter 3:18 we learn that, 'Christ suffered for our sins once for all time. He never sinned, but he died for sinners to bring you safely home to God.'

> *'Christ suffered for our sins once for all time. He never sinned, but he died for sinners to bring you safely home to God.'*

In John 3:16–18 we read Jesus' own explanation of the salvation that he brought the world:

For God loved the world so much that he gave his one and only Son, so that everyone who believes in him will not perish but have eternal life. God sent his Son into the world not to judge the world, but to save the world through him.

There is no judgement against anyone who believes in him. But anyone who does not believe in him has already been judged for not believing in God's one and only Son.

Did you know that the name 'Jesus' – 'Yeshua' in Aramaic (the language Jesus grew up speaking)

— is usually translated as 'God saves'? A more contemporary paraphrase would be 'God-to-the-rescue!' God's amazing act of rescue shows us that he loves us so much that he could not find it in himself to abandon humankind to our own miserable ways. In 1 John 4:16 God is described incredibly simply, 'God is love.' Love had to intervene.

Grace

Christians use this little word to refer to the love of God expressed through Jesus' death on the cross. Someone once helpfully explained grace with the acronym G-R-A-C-E:

God's
Riches
At
Christ's
Expense

Are you ready to believe that Jesus died for you? Are you willing to take a step of faith and accept him as your Saviour?

The New Testament makes it clear that repentance is part of the process we need to go through in order to meet with Jesus.

Repentance

The New Testament makes it clear that repentance is part of the process we need to go through in order to meet with Jesus. After Jesus' resurrection, when people who were convinced about him asked Peter what they needed to do next he said, 'Each of you must repent of your sins and turn to God, and be baptised in the name of Jesus Christ for the forgiveness of your sins. Then you will receive the gift of the Holy Spirit' (Acts 2:38).

The original Greek word for repentance is made up of the two parts: 'change' and 'mind'. When Jesus said: 'Repent of your sins and turn to God' (Matthew 3:2), he wanted his listeners to do more than just say 'sorry' for their mistakes, but also to choose God and turn away from their past. He was asking for a complete change of attitude, which would inevitably lead to a change in lifestyle.

Jesus Offers Free Forgiveness

Sitting on the London tube recently, I noticed the slogan printed on a woman's environmentally friendly fabric bag. It said: 'We are what we do'. It is this philosophy on life that drives humanity into a frenzied attempt at self-justification. It leads to crippling guilt because we know we can never do enough good things to meet God's standards. But if you repent and believe in Jesus you no longer have to try to justify yourself. Earning Brownie points from God becomes pointless.

Have you ever found yourself burdened by feelings of guilt for past mistakes? Followers of Jesus can say goodbye to guilt FOR EVER! Jesus forgives completely and freely. When he looks at you, he sees you as whiter than snow (Psalm 51:7), cleansed and forgiven. Free forgiveness? That sounds too good to be true. It doesn't sound fair, does it, for me to mess up and then to go free? We don't need to worry about whether it is fair. The truth is that Jesus took all our sin and guilt when he was nailed on the cross, simply because he loves us. This is the upside down economy of grace.

I was in my local supermarket recently. When I got to the checkout I noticed that the woman sitting at the till had a cross around her neck. 'You must be a Christian,' I said.

She looked up. 'What?'

'You are wearing a cross around your neck.'

'Oh, it is nice isn't it?'

'It wasn't nice, it was nasty,' I said. The woman looked at me as though I were an alien that had landed from another planet.

'Listen,' I said. 'If I was wearing an earring designed like a gas chamber on one of my ears and another earring designed like an electric chair on the other one, you would think I was crazy. You would ask me why I was wearing such crazy jewellery. I'd say, "Well, I like to remember how millions of Jews died in the Second World War. And I like to remember how certain people were executed for their crimes in the United States."' I asked her what she would think of me then.

> *Jesus didn't just wear the cross around his neck. He carried it on his back.*

'I'd think you'd lost it,' she said.

'Is that because they are symbols of execution?'

I asked her. 'What are you wearing around your neck?'

Jesus didn't just wear the cross around his neck. He carried it on his back. He didn't pay a few quid for it in a jewellery shop – the cross cost him his life. If you are carrying the weight of your guilt, let go of it, accepting that Jesus has already shouldered it for you. In John 14:27 it is recorded that, shortly before his death, Jesus said, 'I am leaving you with a gift – peace of mind and heart. And the peace I give is a gift the world cannot give.' And that is a peace we can still enjoy today, through the power of the Holy Spirit. Is that Good News, or is that Good News?!

Accepting the Freebie

A little boy was standing in Trafalgar Square, London. He was in front of Nelson's Column, and next to him was a policeman. The boy looked up and said, 'I'd like to buy this.'

The policeman asked, 'How much have you got?'

'75p.'

'Well that is not enough to buy Nelson's Column.'

'I thought you'd say that.'

The policeman replied: 'Well, you need to understand three things: 1) you could never afford to buy this monument; 2) it is not for sale; and 3) if you are a British citizen it already belongs to you – it belongs to the people.'

God's forgiveness is like that. It is priceless, and it is ours to enjoy. All we need to do is believe in

Jesus, repent and accept his love for us. In this way we claim what is already ours.

The End is Just the Beginning . . .

As you may know, the life of Jesus did not end with his funeral: three days after he died on the cross, God raised him back to life again. In Acts 2:24 we read: 'God released him from the horrors of death and raised him back to life, for death could not keep him in its grip.' Of course, Jesus is not physically present on earth today because after 40 days of reappearing to people after his death, he rose up into the skies. However, the Spirit of Jesus comes to every person who decides to follow him, enabling us to have a relationship with Jesus.

Jesus explained all this to his disciples even before he was crucified: 'in fact, it is best for you that I go away, because if I don't, the Advocate [helper] won't come. If I do go away, then I will send him to you. And when he comes, he will convict the world of its sin, and of God's righteousness, and of the coming judgement' (John 16:7,8).

Let's take a closer look at the wonderful transformation that starts to take place when you invite Jesus into your life.

Transformation

When I started this process on that historic day on 9 February 1975, it was the most cathartic, therapeutic experience that I've ever had. The light came on. Even my mother noticed a change in me.

Alarmed, she said, 'You have been brainwashed!' My response was quite simple: 'Mum, my brain *has* been washed. If you only knew what was in my brain before, you'd be pleased it got washed.'

> *Don't feel threatened by the idea of a transformation. God won't perform personality replacement surgery on you, he just wants you to become more fully you.*

Don't feel threatened by the idea of a transformation. God won't perform personality replacement surgery on you, he just wants you to become more fully you: more loving, more generous, more thoughtful and more creative. Without the continued assistance of our Creator we deviate from his original plan for us. He longs for you to let him reform you into the person he created you to be in the first place, with all the potential in the world to love him and others as yourself. This process is not like turning over a new leaf or making a New Year's resolution, which fizzles out after a few weeks. The Holy Spirit comes into our hearts to guide and strengthen us every day, so that we are better able to serve God for the rest of our lives.

Get Baptised

Jesus said, 'I tell you the truth, unless you are born again, you cannot see the Kingdom of God . . . I assure you, no one can enter the Kingdom of God without being born of water and the Spirit' (John 3:3–5). What does this mean in practice? Birth by water means being baptised after a declaration of belief in Jesus as Lord. This was the kind of baptism that Jesus' early disciples were carrying out, both during Jesus' lifetime and afterwards in the early days of the church. Jesus said, 'I have been given all authority in heaven and on earth. Therefore, go and make disciples of all the nations, baptising them in the name of the Father and the Son and the Holy Spirit' (Matthew 28:18,19).

Getting baptised in water symbolises the washing away of your sins that takes place when you believe in Jesus and repent. As you rise up out of the baptism pool, you are making a symbolic declaration that you want to leave the old you behind, and embark on a journey of transformation with Jesus.

Resolve to Follow Jesus

If you are about to embark on this journey, you should know that Christianity cannot offer a pick-and-mix solution to spirituality. You can't just believe in the warm and cuddly bits and ignore the more challenging aspects of the Christian faith. Jesus calls his followers to die to their old self and be reborn in him. Jesus said, 'If any of you wants to be my follower, you must turn from your selfish ways, take up your cross, and follow me. If you try to hang on to your life, you will lose it. But if you give up your life for my sake and for the sake of the Good News, you will save it' (Mark 8:34,35). In other words, it is not necessarily going to be easy.

In fact, it won't be long before you realise you are in a fight. In all my favourite movies the good guys fight the bad guys. The devil, who is also called Satan, represents all the forces of evil in the world – he will do all he can to impede your relationship with God. So brace yourself for a bumpy ride. Jesus said, 'You can enter God's Kingdom only through the narrow gate.

> *The devil, who is also called Satan, represents all the forces of evil in the world – he will do all he can to impede your relationship with God.*

The highway to hell is broad, and its gate is wide for the many who choose that way. But the gateway to life is very narrow and the road is difficult, and only a few ever find it' (Matthew 7:13,14).

The Joy of the Journey

Whatever challenges lie ahead, as we step out on this new path with Jesus, he walks beside us and we start to experience a new joy. The Apostle Paul's explanation will help you to view the challenges positively:

> Therefore, since we have been made right in God's sight by faith, we have peace with God because of what Jesus Christ our Lord has done for us. Because of our faith, Christ has brought us into this place of undeserved privilege where we now stand, and we confidently and joyfully look forward to sharing God's glory.
> We can rejoice, too, when we run into problems and trials, for we know that they help us develop endurance.

And endurance develops strength of character, and character strengthens our confident hope of salvation. And this hope will not lead to disappointment. For we know how dearly God loves us, because he has given us the Holy Spirit to fill our hearts with his love. (Romans 5:1–5)

Having complete assurance that his relationship with God was restored gave Paul a deep, confident joy. What could be more important than travelling the journey of your life with God as your companion?

Follow God's Commandments

Jesus said, 'If you ignore the least commandment and teach others to do the same, you will be called the least in the Kingdom of Heaven. But anyone who obeys God's laws and teaches them will be called great in the Kingdom of Heaven' (Matthew 5:19). Jesus also instructed us to 'Teach . . . new disciples to obey all the commands I have given you' (Matthew 28:20).

But what are God's laws? They are basically 'The Ten Commandments', which constitute an ancient God-given code for living, dating from the sixteenth century BC and set out in the Old Testament (Exodus 20:3–17). They are not a suffocating list of 'thou-shalt-nots', but profound and wise instructions for human contentment. Here they are in question format, adapted from the original text in Exodus 20 and updated to include Jesus' commentary on them in Matthew 5:17–48:

1. Do you put God at the centre of your life, where he should be?

2. Do you put anything or anyone else in the place of God in your life?
3. Do you ever use the name of God or Jesus carelessly or insincerely?
4. Do you keep one day free each week, to focus on God and get some much-needed rest?
5. Do you respect and honour your parents? Are you taking care of them or would you, if necessary?
6. Do you ever get so angry with someone that you might as well have killed them? Have you ever killed anybody?
7. Have you ever committed adultery? Do you ever have impure or lustful thoughts about another person?
8. Do you ever steal anything, either big or small, or take anything that doesn't belong to you?
9. Do you ever lie about other people or misrepresent them in any way?
10. Do you ever crave things that don't belong to you?

Some people treat the Ten Commandments a bit like an exam paper: 'Please only attempt five.' But they are not 'The Ten Suggestions', they are God's commandments for brilliant, enjoyable, intelligent living. If you are now resolving to follow Jesus, choose this as your basic framework for living.

> *Some people treat the Ten Commandments a bit like an exam paper: 'Please only attempt five.'*

Getting Practical

Are you having difficulty imagining how a new relationship with Jesus might work in practical terms? How do you eat an elephant? Answer: one bite at a time . . . Inch by inch, everything is a cinch! If your aim is to be healthier, maybe you walk a bit more and take the stairs instead of the lift. If you want to improve your relationships with your family and friends, maybe you decide to spend an hour more each week being with them. If you want to improve your relationship with God, you will do something similar – something that will gradually take you forward. Don't be unrealistic and resolve to spend an hour every day praying, because it is unlikely you will stick to something so extreme. Instead, begin to spend an extra 5 to 15 minutes each day praying and reading your Bible.

An Incredible Destination

If you have begun a relationship with Jesus, then be reassured that you are going to an amazing place. The New Testament makes it clear that if we accept Jesus into our lives, we will one day enter a new world, called heaven. Romans 5:9,10, 'And since we have been made right in God's sight by the blood of Christ, he will certainly save us from God's condemnation. For since our friendship with God was restored by the death of his Son while we were still his enemies, we will certainly be saved through the life of his Son.'

As the reality of an afterlife sinks in, you will notice yourself start to re-calibrate some of your thinking; life will become full of hope. As Christians, we know that we have been redeemed by Jesus' death on the cross, we are being made perfect in the present and in heaven we will become our complete selves. When you introduce this knowledge and exciting reality into your life, it will make you a whole lot happier!

Are you willing to start on the journey towards that heavenly destination? It is the journey that your creator planned for you to take before the beginning of time. His sole intention for you is that you live your life his way, not yours. This is the purpose that God has for your soul; it is your sole purpose.

> *This is the purpose that God has for your soul; it is your sole purpose.*

Three Steps Towards God

If you believe in the message of Jesus and want to begin a relationship with him, take three simple steps now.

1. Admit: acknowledge that you are separated from God. Whether you have consciously rejected him, or just ignored him, admit that you need a mediator who'll step in and mend your broken relationship. Admit, too, that you deserve punishment for your sin.
2. Commit: when you commit your life to Jesus, God forgives you and breathes new life into you. In the physical world, new life is created as soon

as conception takes place, but in the spiritual world new life begins when you commit your life to Jesus. In receiving the Holy Spirit and the new life Jesus offers, you will in effect be 'born again'.

3. Submit: it is one thing to admit that we have sinned and say that we want to start afresh with God by committing ourselves to him. It is quite another to live that relationship out, day by day. By submitting to God, we resolve to live as God wants us to.

Prayer

'Heavenly Father, I admit that I have not kept your commandments and lived as you created me to. Lord Jesus Christ, I commit my life to you. Thank you that you paid the price for my sins so I can be forgiven. Holy Spirit, I submit to your power. Come fill my life with your presence so that I may live to the praise and glory of God. Amen.'

Further Reading

If you are at a place of uncertainty about the message of Jesus, I suggest you try reading some of the following books and websites. They tackle questions often put to the Christian faith and should provide you with some helpful answers (this is sometimes known as 'apologetics'):

If You Could Ask God One Question, Paul Williams and Barry Cooper, Good Book Company, 2007
What Every Christian Should Know, Richard S. Taylor, CWR, 2004

Who Made God? And Answers to Over 100 Other Tough Questions, Ravi Zacharias and Norman Geisler, Zondervan Publishing House, 2003
A Time to Search, Joe Boot, Kingsway Publications, 2002
Don't Check Your Brains at the Door: A Book of Christian Evidences, Josh McDowell and Bob Hostetler, Word Publishing, 1992
www.bethinking.org
www.zactrust.org/resources

2

The Manager

Who Exactly is Jesus Christ?

Legend has it that when the band 'The Who' were trying to find a name for themselves, a few members were hard of hearing. In response to suggestions for names they kept on asking 'The who?' In the end, the name stuck! When you hear the name Jesus, do you ask 'who?' What do you know about the manager of the universe? Creation influences every person on the planet, but they don't always know the name of its Creator. In fact, many people only know the words 'Jesus Christ' as a means of expressing irritation, forgetting – or not realising – that they are talking about the Christ, the Son of God who can forgive our sins and transform our lives.

In John 14:9–11 Jesus said, 'Anyone who has seen me has seen the Father . . . Don't you believe that I am in the Father and the Father is in me? The words I speak are not my own, but my Father who lives in me does his work through me. Just believe that I am in the Father and the Father is in me. Or at least believe because of the work you have seen me do.' Jesus also explained his identity in several other ways – enabling all sorts of people to understand who he was . . .

For the chefs and bakers among us, he said: 'I am the bread of life. Whoever comes to me will never be hungry again. Whoever believes in me will never be thirsty' (John 6:35).

For everyone with a well-tended garden and for those who appreciate a glass of wine, he explained: 'I am the true grapevine, and my Father is the gardener' (John 15:1).

For farmers and animal lovers, he said: 'I am the good shepherd. The good shepherd sacrifices his life for the sheep' (John 10:11).

For all of us used to well-lit offices and multimedia rock concerts, he explained: 'I am the light of the world. If you follow me, you won't have to walk in darkness, because you will have the light that leads to life' (John 8:12).

For the builders and DIY enthusiasts among us, Jesus refers to himself as the cornerstone, the most important stone in a structure. In Luke 20:17,18, he says: 'Everyone who stumbles over that stone will be broken to pieces, and it will crush anyone it falls on.' Later on in Acts 4:11, Luke explains: 'For Jesus is the one referred to in the Scriptures [Psalm 118:22], where it says, "The stone that you builders rejected has now become the cornerstone."'

One of the first disciples, John, explained who Jesus was for the book-lovers and chatterboxes.

> *'In the beginning the Word already existed. The Word was with God, and the Word was God.'*

Introducing Jesus as the 'Word', in John 1:1 he wrote: 'In the beginning the Word already existed. The Word was with God, and the Word was God.' Then in verse 4 he wrote: 'The Word gave life to everything that was created, and his life brought light to everyone.' Then, in verse 14 he explained: 'So the Word became human and made his home among us.'

Most importantly, for those of us who tend to get lost in one-way systems or who are overly dependent on maps, Jesus explained: 'I am the way, the truth, and the life. No one can come to the Father except through me' (John 14:6).

Saint, Sissy or Samson?

What kind of image comes to mind when you think of Jesus? Some people think: 'Oh, yeah, gentle Jesus, meek and mild. Long blond hair, beard, blue eyes . . .' They picture Jesus dressed in a fluffy white dressing gown. Actually, he wasn't like that at all. Jesus was the toughest, most resilient man that ever lived; yet he was also the most loving, caring and compassionate man ever to have walked on the earth. Jesus was a fascinating, awe-inspiring, outspoken man. In this chapter we will take a closer look at his remarkable life story – and consider its relevance to you and me today.

Jesus to the Rescue!

Nowadays, a plethora of self-help books claiming to fix every imaginable human problem are available. This can make it hard to believe the Bible's message that without Jesus, every single person on the planet is in a serious, helpless predicament. We need a lot more than determination, initiative and self-confidence to get out of the mess we find ourselves in when we try to live without God. No self-help book can or could possibly even come close to providing a solution. Our world needs a rescuer.

The Hero

One of my favourite movies is the classic *Superman*. It is the concept of the unlikely superhero that grabs me – somehow we can all relate to the normality of Clark Kent, who one minute is working as a journalist, and the next is able to throw on his blue tights, red pants and save the world.

At the time of writing of the end of the Old Testament, the idea of a heroic person, a Messiah who would rescue the human race, was a familiar one. At the time of Jesus' birth, Jews were looking forward to the coming of their Messiah, the king who would save them from all

At the time of Jesus' birth, Jews were looking forward to the coming of their Messiah, the king who would save them from all their enemies.

their enemies. Numerous people had even prophesied about how and when this rescuer would appear. In the Old Testament, people are often described as being lost sheep, so the Messiah was described as a shepherd. In Ezekiel 34:1–16, God pronounces judgement on the people's leaders, saying they are like failing shepherds. Then he says:

> 'I will rescue my flock from their mouths . . . I myself will search and find my sheep. I will be like a shepherd looking for his scattered flock. I will find my sheep and rescue them from all the places where they were scattered . . . I myself will tend my sheep and give them a place to lie down in peace . . . I will search for my lost ones who strayed away, and I will bring them safely home again. I will bandage the injured and strengthen the weak.'

The repetition of the word 'I' is striking: God is promising here that he, personally, will bring back the lost sheep. In the New Testament, Jesus picks up this prophecy and applies it to himself. In John 10:11 he says: 'I am the good shepherd. The good shepherd sacrifices his life for the sheep.'

The message of the Bible is that God personally came to rescue us, and that he did this through Jesus. Just as Clark Kent seems an unlikely super-hero, so the humble person of Jesus, born into a lowly family in an insignificant place, was a surprising Saviour. Jesus did not come to earth as a comfortable man of the twenty-first century, cushioned by the health service, central heating, antibiotics and dentists. The unlikely hero came into a life of poverty, pain and manual labour.

His Birth

You have probably heard of the virgin birth. It should really be called the virgin conception. If you believe in God, the idea that he could create life in a woman who has not had sex should not be outrageous. The fact that Jesus came to this world as a baby, not as some apparition, is important because it indicates that Jesus was definitely a human being. After all, to be human means being born as a baby. Mary gave birth to Jesus in a place called Bethlehem (now in the Palestinian West Bank, in the Middle East) but she and Joseph, her new husband, could find no lodging there. We read in Luke 2:7: 'She wrapped [the baby] snugly in strips of cloth and laid him in a manger, because there was no lodging available for them'.

> *The fact that Jesus came to this world as a baby, not as some apparition, is important because it indicates that Jesus was definitely a human being.*

The Gospel of Matthew (1:1–17) records that the baby Jesus was a descendant of both King David and Abraham, making him Jewish. Luke 3:23–38 records that his ancestry went right back to Adam, to make the point that he was a normal member of the human race. These facts occurred just as the Old Testament prophecies had predicted.

Luke records that some local shepherds visited the new family after being told by an angel that the Messiah had just been born (Luke 2:8–20). These shepherds then went and spread the news about the arrival of the long-awaited Saviour. Notice that it was shepherds – people close to the bottom of the social ladder – who were given this honour. Perhaps Luke included this detail to remind his readers this baby was to be Good News for the poor and those on the margins of society, not just the rich and powerful. To Jesus all people would matter, even those in the humblest jobs, living on the very edges of society.

The child Jesus was also visited by three men who were called 'wise'. These men really understood who Jesus was and why he had come. It is probably thanks to the wise men that we now give presents at Christmas – although with Jesus in the picture Christmas becomes more than just a time to give presents!

December 25th is only an arbitrary date for celebrating the birth of Jesus. We can deduce that Jesus was born no earlier than 6 BC and no later than 4 BC. We know from history that it was Constantine, the first Christian Roman Emperor (who ruled in AD 336), who decided that the former pagan mid-winter festival should be turned into a Christian celebration to commemorate Jesus' birth.

His Life

We know very little about Jesus' early life. Soon after his birth, his mother Mary and step-father Joseph fled to Egypt. King Herod, the political leader in the area at the time, had met with the wise men and heard their story about the birth of an amazing new king. Feeling his own position was under threat, he then ordered the massacre of all infants of two years and under. Not long afterwards, Mary and Joseph settled in Nazareth, a small village in a remote northern part of Palestine (now Israel). As a result, Jesus would have grown up speaking with a heavy (and much mocked) Galilee accent.

In his teens, Jesus learnt his father's trade of carpentry; he would have worn normal worker's clothes. He probably would have had the leathery, scarred hands of any labourer in the developing world today. Jesus would have been like everyone else in a crowd until he started his ministry. The only thing that would have marked him out was an unusual devotion to God and his Word, but his humility was such that he would not have paraded this.

> *In his teens,*
> *Jesus learnt his*
> *father's trade*
> *of carpentry; he*
> *would have worn*
> *normal worker's*
> *clothes.*

Miraculous Powers

It seems that Jesus performed his first recorded miracle a little against his will. His mother, Mary, was clearly well aware of his powers when she asked him to help out by turning water into wine at a wedding they were attending (John 2:1–11). We can only assume that she must have witnessed some interesting things during his childhood!

The Big Three Zero

According to Luke 3:1–3, John the Baptist began to preach in AD 27. Jesus started teaching soon afterwards, which would make him about 30 years old when he started his ministry (Luke 3:23). It may seem incredible that Jesus would have been content to simply work as a carpenter until this time, however, we must remember that 30 was thought a significant age in the Old Testament. Joseph (the one with the amazing dream coat) was 30 when he started serving the King of Egypt (Genesis 41:46) and David was 30 when he started reigning over Judah (2 Samuel 5:4). This was also considered the best age for priests to start working in the temple (Numbers 4:3). Jesus' ministry began at a deeply significant time.

Baptism and Wilderness

Before Jesus began to teach, he went to be baptised by John, who was baptising numerous people in the River Jordan (Luke 3:21). As the baptism took place, we are told that: 'The heavens opened, and the Holy Spirit, in bodily form, descended on [Jesus] like a dove. And a voice from heaven said, "You are my dearly beloved Son, and you bring me great joy"' (Luke 3:22).

After being baptised, Jesus went to spend forty days in the wilderness. There, while he was fasting, he was tempted by the devil in various ways, but of course he resisted each time, quoting passages from the Old Testament. When he was tempted to turn a stone into bread, he said: 'No! The Scriptures say, "People do not live by bread alone."' When told he could have authority over all the kingdoms of this world, if he would worship the Devil, Jesus said, 'The Scriptures say, "You must worship the Lᴏʀᴅ your God and serve only him"'. And when he was invited to throw himself off a high point, to prove that God would send angels to save him from harm, he said, 'The Scriptures also say, "You must not test the Lᴏʀᴅ your God"' (Luke 4:1–13). After this, Jesus started teaching immediately and people everywhere were amazed by what he said.

Teacher and Healer

We can deduce that Jesus taught for about three years before he died. Three phases can be identified during his teaching ministry. In the first phase he was based in Judea (the southern part of modern Palestine). He only had a few disciples during this period, on a very informal basis. Interestingly, the men he asked to 'Come, follow me' (see Matthew 4:18–22) were not the movers and shakers of the time – they were simple, financially poor fishermen. Right from the start of his ministry, Jesus spent time with the poor, the sick and the outcasts of society – he smashed social taboos by touching and healing a leper (Matthew 8:1–4), talking to a Samaritan woman (John 4:1–26) and dining with a despised tax collector (Luke 19:1–9). During this first phase, Jesus performed

Right from the start of his ministry, Jesus spent time with the poor.

miracles and made reference in his teaching to his coming death and resurrection.

In the second phase of his ministry, Jesus was based in Galilee. Having been rejected by the religious leaders in Jerusalem in the first period of his teaching, we now find him inviting twelve men to become his disciples. During this phase, Jesus preached publicly on a large scale, in particular explaining to his followers that he had come to bring in the 'Kingdom of Heaven'. This, he said, was the wonderful reign of God over all the earth – and he described it using many parables (or riddles) to help people understand what he meant. Once he said: 'The Kingdom of Heaven is like a treasure that a man discovered hidden in a field. In his excitement, he hid it again and sold everything he owned to get enough money to buy the field' (Matthew 13:44).

Jesus enjoyed incredible popularity during this second phase of his ministry – enormous crowds followed him around and people suffering from any kind of physical or mental complaint sought him out to be cured. He performed numerous miracles and clearly outraged people at times, too. Once, so many were angry with him that he had to escape. He did so by simply slipping through the crowd (Luke 4:28–30).

In the third phase of his ministry, Jesus revealed fully that he was not the kind of king his followers had imagined. The Jews had traditionally hoped for a warrior king who would crush their political enemies – but instead Jesus was to show them that he was one with God, and reigned over all things, including death. Jesus warned his disciples that he would eventually suffer a terrible fate at the hands of the religious leaders (Mark 8:31). He also gave the news (which was no doubt disturbing) that the

> *The Jews had traditionally hoped for a warrior king who would crush their political enemies.*

disciples would also have to suffer, saying: 'If any of you wants to be my follower, you must turn from your selfish ways, take up your cross, and follow me. If you try to hang on to your life, you will lose it. But if you give up your life for my sake, you will save it' (Matthew 16:24,25).

The Messiah

About a week after this a mysterious thing happened. Three of the disciples were suddenly given the opportunity to see Jesus in all his divine glory. He became transfigured in front of them (Matthew 17:1 9). Moses and Elijah represent the two great divisions of the Old Testament, the Law and the Prophets. The transfiguration was similar to Moses' meeting with God on Mount Sinai (Exodus 19) and the cloud was like that often associated with God's presence in the Old Testament. For a moment these three men had seen Jesus in all his glory, majesty and honour. This event must have proved to the disciples that Jesus was indeed God, as he claimed. Here was the man who would fulfil all the Old Testament prophecies about a coming Messiah.

From this time on, Jesus sought out privacy in order to teach his disciples. He soon took them away from Galilee and moved south to Judea and the adjacent area of Perea. After teaching them for a while there, he moved on to Jerusalem where he clearly knew he would face arrest, trial and execution.

His Death

The Jewish authorities' dislike of Jesus had been escalating for some time. Not only were they irritated by his minor infractions of the Jewish law (he healed people on the Sabbath), but they had also become incensed by his habit of telling people that their sins were forgiven (Matthew 9:1–8). Tensions rose further when he went so far as to raise someone from the dead (John 11:30–44). As Lazarus, the man he raised, was not only very firmly dead but also decomposing, this was sensational and could not be overlooked. This young upstart was clearly about to replace the well-established Jewish leaders simply by astounding people with miracles and other good works. It was decided he would have to be killed. Jesus entered Jerusalem on what we call 'Palm Sunday' and over the next few days the political temperature continued to rise. Finally, with the help of the disciple Judas Iscariot, Jesus was arrested on the eve of the Passover feast.

Jesus faced his future calmly. After a series of speedy sham trials, the brutal but weak Roman Governor Pontius Pilate was persuaded to have this 'King of the Jews' crucified. (The temple leaders did not have the authority to organise this for themselves.) The Bible records some mysterious events occurring on the day Jesus was crucified. Darkness fell across the land between noon and 3 p.m. (Matthew 27:45, Mark 15:33 and Luke 23:44). 'At the same time, the curtain in the sanctuary of the Temple was torn in two, from top to bottom. The earth shook, rocks split apart and tombs opened. The bodies of many men and women who had died were raised from the dead. They left the cemetery after Jesus' resurrection, went into the holy city of Jerusalem, and appeared to many people. These strange happenings terrified the Roman officer and the other soldiers at the crucifixion.

> *The earth shook, rocks split apart and tombs opened. The bodies of many men and women who had died were raised from the dead.*

They said, "This man truly was the Son of God!"' (Matthew 27:51–54). Perhaps these events suggest both God's judgement falling across the land and also that – through the symbolism of the curtain tearing open – the way to God was no longer restricted. Jesus had truly paid the price of sin, which up until that point had separated humanity from God.

Jesus' body was taken down from the cross by a wealthy sympathiser and buried in a stone cave. With anyone else, that would have been that: birth, life, death and burial – the whole cradle-to-grave experience. But not for Jesus . . .

His Resurrection

Three days after Jesus died on the cross, God raised him back to life. Christians believe he is still alive today, and that we can communicate with him and through him find forgiveness, direction and purpose for our lives.

In Mark 16:9–20, we can read an account of what happened:

After Jesus rose from the dead early on Sunday morning, the first person who saw him was Mary Magdalene, the woman from whom he had cast out seven demons. She went to the disciples, who were grieving and weeping, and told them what had happened. But when she told them that Jesus was alive and she had seen him, they didn't believe her.

Afterward he appeared in a different form to two of his followers who were walking from Jerusalem into the country. They rushed back to tell the others, but no one believed them.

Still later he appeared to the eleven disciples as they were eating together. He rebuked them for their stubborn unbelief because they refused to believe those who had seen him after he had been raised from the dead.

And then he told them, 'Go into all the world and preach the Good News to everyone. Anyone who believes and is baptised will be saved. But anyone who refuses to believe will be condemned. These miraculous signs will accompany those who believe: They will cast out demons in my name, and they will speak in new languages. They will be able to handle snakes with safety, and if they drink anything poisonous, it won't hurt them. They will be able to place their hands on the sick, and they will be healed.'

When the Lord Jesus had finished talking with them, he was taken up into heaven and sat down in the place of honour at God's right hand. And the disciples went everywhere and preached, and the Lord worked through them, confirming what they said by many miraculous signs.

In Acts 1:3 we are told that after his death, Jesus appeared to his disciples (now called apostles) from time to time, proving to them that he was truly alive. He also spent time talking to them about the kingdom of God over this period. In 1 Corinthians 15:6 the apostle Paul tells us that at one point the resurrected Jesus was seen by more than five hundred of his followers at once – hardly the stuff of a hallucination. Amazingly, these appearances continued for forty days after Jesus' death!

> *Jesus appeared to his disciples (now called apostles) from time to time, proving to them that he was truly alive.*

Sometimes people ask me, 'Why Jesus? Why not another philosophy or religion?' Imagine for a moment that you are walking down a road. You come to a junction and you don't know which way to go. Then you see two men lying on the ground: one dead and one alive. Who do you ask for directions? The reason I'm a Christian is because Jesus rose from the dead and can still give us direction today.

What Was the Resurrected Jesus Like?

From the reports of eyewitnesses, two statements can be made about the resurrected Christ:

- The appearances were of Jesus himself, as his body bore the evidence of crucifixion and the spear wound to the chest. Jesus also had the same personal relationship with his followers as he had done before his death. Yet, there were also changes that meant that an immediate identification of him was not always made.
- The appearances were real and physical. The writers of the New Testament are at pains to make it clear that this was no delusion. The risen Jesus allowed himself to be touched, embraced and he ate food, specifically to make the point that he was not a ghost. Yet he passed through walls and locked doors. The accounts suggest a new, and so far unique, form of existence, with similarities and differences to ordinary human life. But then, given who Jesus was, something unique would not be surprising.

What Was the Point of the Resurrection?

The logic of the resurrection, although never spelled out in the Bible, is like this: death is a result of sin, therefore sinless people cannot stay dead. However, what had been a theoretical possibility (there had been no sinless people before) became a reality with Jesus, proving him to be the Christ, the Messiah predicted so many times in the Old Testament. As Peter

The resurrection is vitally important because it authenticates everything Jesus said and did.

said in Acts 2:24: 'death could not keep him in its grip'.

The resurrection is vitally important because it authenticates everything Jesus said and did. It is hard to exaggerate the significance of this event – it changes everything for quite a few reasons:

- it confirms that God considered Jesus sinless, and that he was all he claimed to be. After a death considered so shameful by the Jews, this was important. By rising from the dead, Jesus showed that he was in control of death, sin and Satan. In other words, the resurrection shows that he really is Lord of everything;
- it shows that Satan's rule of this planet is limited – Jesus is more powerful than Satan;
- it signals the incoming of God's kingdom, which Jesus taught about during his time on earth.

To Heaven

After Jesus had appeared to people over a short period of time, he returned to heaven in an event known as 'the ascension'. In Luke 24:50–53 (NIV) we read: 'When he had led them out to the vicinity of Bethany, he lifted up his hands and blessed them. While he was blessing them, he left them and was taken up into heaven. Then they worshipped him and returned to Jerusalem with great joy. And they stayed continually at the temple, praising God.' The ascension visibly demonstrated to the disciples the end of Jesus' earthly ministry, and prepared the way for the coming of the Holy Spirit at Pentecost.

Some people have been puzzled by the idea of Jesus ascending into some sort of physical heaven 'up there', which not even the Hubble space telescope has managed to find. Perhaps we should stop looking and instead follow the lead of modern physics and sci-fi films and try to think of heaven as existing in some sort of parallel dimension to our world. We will look in more detail at what heaven is in the final chapter of this book.

Without the resurrection, the church would not have been born and certainly would never have survived. Without the ascension, the power of the Spirit would never have been given to the disciples. And it was only through the power of the Spirit that this group of straggly, demoralised no-hopers was transformed into serious leaders. They were not only able to perform the miracles Jesus himself had demonstrated – they even had the dynamism and energy to take the message of Christianity to thousands of people and establish thriving churches wherever they went. It is no wonder, then, that the resurrection is considered the cornerstone of Christianity.

Is Jesus Really Relevant Today?

What is the significance for us today of Jesus' outrageous life, so filled with courage, love, power and self-sacrifice? Jesus was not just a wacky guy with an unusual life. He was God, living on earth as a human. Jesus was and is the embodiment of love and truth. Jesus overcame death, sin and evil by dying on the cross and being raised again to life. Jesus' resurrection makes eternal life possible for you and for me. He has made it possible for us to have a future with him full of joy, peace, forgiveness and hope.

> *He has made it possible for us to have a future with him full of joy, peace, forgiveness and hope.*

Are You Under New Management?

Today, Jesus wants to come into your life and be your friend and manager. You just need to let him in. If you do, or have recently done so, three things will happen.

1. Your past will be forgiven

I received a letter from a man who wrote this: 'I'm 34 years old and divorced, though I fought the divorce and I feel bad. I have no hope for my future. Often I go home and cry but there is no one holding me when I do. No one cares. Nothing changes and I continue to fail. I am stressed out emotionally and I feel on the verge of collapse. Something is very wrong but I feel so hurt and embittered that I can scarcely react or relate to others any more. I feel as though I'm going to sit out the rest of my life in the penalty box.'

The tragedy is there are so many people like that in our world. People who can't get on with the present or the future because they are stuck in the past. They can't come to terms with what has happened. Guilt, regret or some other negative emotion has tied them down. I replied to that letter with the message that the past really can be the past. And the same goes for you. Each of us can have our past forgiven if we want to – because of what Jesus did for us on the cross. He was nailed to a cross, so that you and I can stop nailing ourselves.

2. *Your current problems will become manageable*

Much of life seems unmanageable when we don't have Jesus to help. But because of the resurrection, God's power can strengthen us to face whatever life throws at us. Maturity comes when we figure out that we can't have it all figured out. When you realise this and are in a position to say, 'God, please help me', he will. That is the Good News – God really does want to help us and we can now communicate directly with him to ask him to do so.

Just before he died, Jesus clearly said to the disciples:

'I tell you the truth, anyone who believes in me will do the same works I have done, and even greater works, because I am going to be with the Father. You can ask for anything in my name, and I will do it, so that the Son can bring glory to the Father. Yes, ask me for anything in my name, and I will do it!' (John 14:12–14)

> *Many people say that they feel powerless to change a situation or break a bad habit.*

Many people say that they feel powerless to change a situation or break a bad habit. They don't see how they can mend a broken relationship, gain self-confidence or get out of debt. To deal with issues like these, we need a power that is greater than ourselves. In Ephesians 1:19– 22, Paul talks about this power. He says:

> I also pray that you will understand the incredible greatness of God's power for us who believe him. This is the same mighty power that raised Christ from the dead and seated him in the place of honour at God's right hand in the heavenly realms. Now he is far above any ruler or authority or power or leader or anything else – not only in this world but also in the world to come. God has put all things under the authority of Christ and has made him head over all things for the benefit of the church.

If you accept Jesus as manager of your life, the power of the Holy Spirit will start to work within you. Through him your problems, responsibilities and worries can be dealt with. By the power of the Spirit your life can be renewed and restored.

3. *Your prospects will improve*

With Jesus as your manager, you will feel a new optimism about the future. Your future will be secure not only in this life, but also after you die. If you put yourself in Jesus' hands you will be able to face death with confidence.

Did you know that the Australian coat of arms pictures two creatures – the emu, a flightless bird, and the kangaroo? The animals were chosen because they share a characteristic that appealed to Australian citizens. Both the emu and kangaroo can move only forward, not back. The emu's three-toed foot causes it to fall if it tries to go backwards, and the kangaroo is prevented from moving in reverse by its large tail. Those who truly choose to follow Jesus are like the emu and kangaroo, moving only forward, never back.

Going Through with the Handover

Have you ever been on a tour of a castle? In the throne room there is always a seat for one. Thrones come in all shapes, sizes and styles but they all share one thing in common: they are made for one occupant. Decide to have Jesus on the throne of your life and make sure that nothing and no one else jostles for his space.

In a recent interview in *The Guardian*, interior designers Justin and Colin shared their views on shopping. Justin was asked: 'Does shopping make you happy?' He answered: 'Shopping is the elixir of life. If ever anything is wrong – within reason – there is nothing that lifts a mood better than a wander down your local high street . . .' In Matthew 6:24 it is recorded that Jesus said: 'No one can serve two masters. For you will hate one and love the other; you will be devoted to one and despise the other. You cannot serve both God and money.' Perhaps your own master is not money, or shopping, but something else. Is there

> '*No one can serve two masters. For you will hate one and love the other; you will be devoted to one and despise the other.*'

something in your life distracting you from God, or preventing you from handing over management of your life to him?

If you allow Jesus to become your new manager, he will manage you like no other – in tenderness, grace and truth. He will give you his power, peace and wisdom. With time, you will become increasingly aware of his limitless love for you, and the freedom that only he can offer.

Prayer

'Lord Jesus, you are my king, my healer, my leader, my creator, my goal, my God and my Saviour. I cannot live without you. I hand over authority to you to manage every area of my life. Amen.'

Further Reading

The Life: A Portrait of Jesus, J.John and Chris Walley, Authentic Lifestyle, 2006

What's So Amazing About Grace? Philip Yancey, Zondervan Publishing House, 2002

The Case for Christ, Lee Strobel, Zondervan Publishing House, 1998

The Jesus I Never Knew, Philip Yancey, Zondervan Publishing House, 2002

The Empty Cross of Jesus, Michael Green, Kingsway Publications, 2005

www.rejesus.com

3

The Manual

What Manual?

Do you have a Bible? If so, you own a compact library with the potential to transform your life. Imagine how awkward it would be if you arrived in heaven having not read the Bible . . .

Peter says, 'Welcome! We have been expecting you.' He ushers you in and continues, 'Let me introduce you to Obadiah.'

Obadiah says, 'What did you think of my book?'

You say, 'I'm sorry, who published it?' As you make your excuses, Zephaniah approaches you.

'What did you think of my book?' he says. 'Did you like it?'

Next you meet Micah . . .

The Maker's Manual

A small boy wandered into his grandfather's empty study. As he entered, he noticed a chess set laid out on a low table. Twenty minutes later, his grandfather returned to the study to find a fortress of books constructed on his carpet, and chess pieces set up all over the floor. The boy had formed the black and white pieces into two armies setting out to battle.

'Ah, grandson,' he said, gently removing a knight from the boy's hand and putting it back in its position on the board. 'The pieces belong on the board. This is an age old game – known by people from all around the world.' Then the old man began rifling through some papers in a drawer, pulling out a weather-beaten instruction manual. 'Let me show you how to play, and we will have a game together.'

I like to think of life as a game. In the game of life we have been given all the pieces, but we don't necessarily know how to play according to the maker's manual. Like the small boy, without direction, each one of us makes up our own game, using the pieces provided. The trouble is, when we make up our own rules in life, other people always end up getting hurt. Integral to the maker of the game of life are the values of love, justice, freedom and equality. We all know how one person's selfish slant on the game of life can cause the suffering of other players.

> *When we make up our own rules in life, other people always end up getting hurt.*

A game with no instruction manual and no rules is not only meaningless, it is also dangerous and not much fun. Imagine a football game with no referee and no goals, a hockey game where you could hit the other players as well as the ball, or a boxing match with no judge and no rounds. Life is no exception – it needs its maker's manual in order for us to be able to get the very best from it.

A Moral God

The Bible tells us of a God who made the world with boundaries: a moral God who justly distinguishes right from wrong. His moral code is neatly summed up in the commandment (which Jesus said was above all other commandments) that we should love God with all our heart and soul and mind, and love our neighbours as ourselves. The instructions that God gives us in the maker's manual all revolve around the concept expressed in this commandment – that we should keep God at the centre of our life. If we do this we will have the strength to participate in life with freedom and fulfilment – not by hurting people, but by helping others and putting them before ourselves. When a parent says to her child: 'Don't touch the cooker! It is hot,' she says this to protect her child – not because she wants to stop him having fun. The Bible is not a simplistic cold-hearted rule book but it does offer the wisdom needed to work out what it means to follow Christ daily in our world.

Did you know that rapper LL Cool J is really called James Smith, Snoop Doggy Dogg is really called Calvin Broadus, and Vanilla Ice is really Robert Van Winkle? Things are not always as they seem. People will tell you that the Bible is nothing but a list of 'do's and don'ts' – read it and you will discover that it is in fact the recipe for a truly satisfying life.

Get to Know Your Maker

Although numerous intellectuals throughout history have found the Christian faith rational and credible, scientists and theologians alike agree that we cannot be entirely scientific in approaching God. We need God to speak to us in order to know him. The primary way that God speaks is through the Bible. It is logical: if you want to know the maker, you have got to read his manual.

> *We need God to speak to us in order to know him.*

What is it exactly?

The Bible is the world's best-selling book. It is, in fact, a collection of 66 books, which are divided into two parts – the Old Testament and the New. It contains nearly a million words in no less than 1,189 chapters; 929 in the Old Testament and 260 in the New Testament. It is packed with wisdom, advice, caution, warning, encouragement, guidance and inspiration. It may cause you to wonder, but it will never cause you to wander!

The Bible was written over a 1,500-year time span, from 1,400 BC to AD 100. It was co-authored by more than forty people who came from all walks of life – kings, peasants, philosophers, physicians, fishermen, poets, statesmen and scholars. They lived in various places, in different political climates and between them they experienced times of war and peace. They were on wildly different wavelengths, lived on three different continents (Asia, Africa and Europe) and wrote in three different languages (Hebrew, Aramaic and Greek).

Centuries ago, translations were a hot political issue and you may be interested to know that the sixteenth-century Bible translators even gave their lives to provide the scriptures in English. At least most of us today have no problem getting hold of a Bible in a language that we can understand.

Many authors, one message

Despite the Bible's length, varied authorship and history, it does have a unified message, which is meaningful and powerful, even today. And it is a message that is relevant to our past, present and future. In summary, it says we can enjoy forgiveness for our past (thanks to Jesus), that we can experience new life today (thanks to the power of the Holy Spirit) and finally that we have hope for the future (thanks to the Father, Son and Holy Spirit). Everything in the Bible is commentary on these three things in one way or another, or is designed to help us understand this basic three-fold message. In the New Testament we are told that: 'these [things] are written so that you may continue to believe that Jesus is the Messiah, the Son of God, and that by believing in him you will have life by the power of his name' (John 20:31).

Perhaps so as to communicate its message clearly and powerfully (and not surprisingly considering the range of authorship) the Bible is written in a variety of different styles. In the Old Testament:

- seventeen of the books are purely historical (Genesis, Exodus, Leviticus, Numbers, Deuteronomy, Joshua, Judges, Ruth, 1 Samuel, 2 Samuel, 1 Kings, 2 Kings, 1 Chronicles, 2 Chronicles, Ezra, Nehemiah and Esther);
- five books are poetical (Job, Psalms, Proverbs, Ecclesiastes and the Song of Solomon);
- seventeen books are prophetic, i.e. they are written by prophets (Isaiah, Jeremiah, Lamentations, Ezekiel, Daniel, Hosea, Joel, Amos, Obadiah, Jonah, Micah, Nahum, Habakkuk, Zephaniah, Haggai, Zechariah and Malachi).

Writing styles in the New Testament are less varied:

- the first four books are accounts of the life, death and resurrection of Jesus (Matthew, Mark, Luke and John);
- after the book of Acts, the next twenty-one books are letters to different churches and individuals (Romans, 1 Corinthians, 2 Corinthians, Galatians, Ephesians, Philippians, Colossians, 1 Thessalonians, 2 Thessalonians, 1 Timothy, 2 Timothy, Titus, Philemon, Hebrews, James, 1 Peter, 2 Peter, 1 John, 2 John, 3 John and Jude);

- the final book in the New Testament, Revelation, is full of intriguing and wonderful prophecies, which few understand and many people argue over!

Two parts, one book

How do we know that the Old and the New Testaments belong together, especially given the 500-year gap between the end of the Old Testament and the beginning of the New? The first chapter of Matthew (at the beginning of the New Testament) clearly links together the two parts of the Bible through the genealogy of Jesus (family tree). Other links are made in the Gospel accounts when the writers explain how Jesus fulfilled the Old Testament prophecies, and both Jesus and the writers of the epistles (letters) in the rest of the New Testament repeatedly refer back to 'scripture', meaning the Old Testament.

> *Themes that run through the entire Bible also indicate that this book sits together as an integrated whole.*

Themes that run through the entire Bible also indicate that this book sits together as an integrated whole. Its contents can, however, be broken down into some broad themes.

- The Old Testament teaches us that there is one, true God. It tells us about many different aspects of his character and shows us how to live in a way that is pleasing to him.

- As we have already mentioned, the first four books of the New Testament (known as the Gospels) focus on Jesus: his life, death, resurrection and teaching are presented from the differing perspectives Matthew, Mark, Luke and John.
- The next book, Acts, which was written by Luke, explains how the Christian church started to grow.
- The twenty-one letters that make up the bulk of the New Testament were written to churches and individuals to guide them in the early days – they remain a brilliant guide for how to be part of church today.
- The last book of the Bible, Revelation, is an encouragement to look beyond the present to what God has in store for his people.

What's Stopping You?

Dr Lockeridge, a charismatic American minister who preached during the late twentieth century, used to tell a story about the Bible. Preparing for a long trip, a traveller told his friend: 'I'm just about packed. I only have to put in a guidebook, a lamp, a mirror, a microscope, a telescope, a volume of fine poetry, a few biographies, a package of old letters, a book of songs, a sword, a hammer and a set of books I've been studying.' This seemed a tall order to the friend.

> *There are various things that can keep us from reading the Bible effectively.*

'You can't get all that into your bag!' he said.

'Yes I can,' the traveller replied. 'It doesn't take much room.' He picked up his Bible and packed it away.

Dr Lockeridge clearly recognised what a useful volume the Bible was and still is for us today. Have you started reading yours?

There are various things that can keep us from reading the Bible effectively. We will consider each one in more detail below.

1. We may put ourselves above the authority of the Bible.
2. We may be dismissive of history and therefore consider the Bible irrelevant.
3. We may no longer value book-based learning.
4. We may assume that accepting Jesus is the last step, rather than the first.

1. Authority

We need to consider the approach that we take in engaging with the Bible. As we read, do we choose to put ourselves above it, reading merely with a critical eye? Or do we see ourselves as being under the authority of the Word of God? Endemic to our culture is a sense that we should distrust any sort of authority – and so to submit to the authority of the Bible can initially feel uncomfortable. But when we read with an open mind, willing to accept that perhaps the wisdom and truth in this book are more advanced than our own, we will begin to find the most incredible things on its pages.

If we accept that this book really is the Word of God, we are submitting to God's authority in submitting to it. Because the Bible is God's own word, it is deeply powerful. In Hebrews 4:12 we read: 'For the word of God is alive and powerful. It is sharper than the sharpest two-edged sword, cutting between soul and spirit, between joint and marrow. It exposes our innermost thoughts and desires.' If we reject the authority of the Bible this would mean choosing the fallible authority of our own minds or of the secular world's over that of God's.

2. History and relevance

Nowadays, our appreciation of history is limited. When asked who the British were fighting in the Battle of Britain, more than one in three young people had no idea that the Germans were the enemy. This ignorance of history is unfortunate because in order to understand the Bible we need to have an understanding of the past. Consider the biblical theme of sheep . . .

When did you last shoo a flock of sheep along a road? When did you last have a chat with a shepherd? The New Testament is packed with references to sheep but the fact is, most of us simply never come into contact with these animals in our urban twenty-first century lives (not to mention goats, donkeys or fishermen). The reason that sheep are such a popular Bible topic is simply because at the time of writing, being a shepherd was a normal job that everybody could relate to. This biblical theme might seem irrelevant today, but with a little research into the historical context in which the Bible was written, we can quickly make sense of it. In Isaiah 40:8 we are reminded: 'The grass withers and the flowers fade, but the word of our God stands forever.' Do you need to reassess your attitude towards history in order to engage with this ancient book?

3. The value of books

Our culture is one of continuous background noise, music, activity and experience. We read less than any generation before us and most reading takes place online. However, the book that God has provided is worth taking time to read because it allows us access to God's truth – and let's face it, much of the material out there for us to read is far from truthful!

> *We love to watch, read and hear about authentic, gritty human life.*

In 1999 the first series of reality TV show *Big Brother* was shown in the Netherlands. There are now six special pan-regional versions of the show aired on TV across the globe. We love to watch, read and hear about authentic, gritty human life. The Bible is a documentary of humanity that gets up close and personal with all sorts of individuals. It was written by a truly earthy, vulnerable collection of people. It is not surprising, then, that it may evoke tears and laughter, repulsion or admiration. This book will keep you thinking for weeks.

4. First or last step?

It might surprise you to read that asking Jesus into your life is not the last step on the journey to God. In fact, it is the first. You have begun a journey of discovery – and just as a plant needs light, oxygen and water to grow, so you too will need to gradually get to know Jesus better by reading the Bible, growing through prayer and meeting other Christians at a local church. The Bible is one aspect of the journey; one that will help you to transform your thoughts, words and actions so that your life is increasingly in alignment with God's will. In 2 Timothy 3:16,17 we learn that: 'All Scripture is inspired by God and is useful to teach us what is true and to make us realise what is wrong in our lives. It corrects us when we are wrong and teaches us to do what is right. God uses it to prepare and equip his people to do every good work.' In other words, if your Bible is falling apart, then you won't be. Someone once said, 'The Bible will keep you from sin, just as sin will keep you from the Bible.'

What the Bible Can Do for You

So far in this chapter we have looked at the basics of the Bible and why it makes a great read. Beyond this, we can use four words to help us understand the role the Bible can have in our lives: find, filter, fix and feed.

The Bible helps us to find the way

A man and his son were swimming in a bay when a mist rolled in. Unable to find their way back to shore, sadly they were drowned. They had been a few yards from safety but died because they didn't know where they were or in which direction to swim for shore. The Bible helps us to find our position in life, just as satellite technology can help us with directions. Think of the Bible as your spiritual sat nav. In Psalm 119:105 we read: 'Your word is a lamp to guide my feet and a light for my path.'

> *Right now you may feel resistant to the idea of finding out where you are in life, but believe me, you really do need to know.*

Right now you may feel resistant to the idea of finding out where you are in life, but believe me, you really do need to know. How can you work out where you are going if you don't know where you are starting out? And part of knowing who you are and where you are, is to find out who God is. The Bible is our main source of God data: reading it reveals where he is and where we are in relation to him.

To give you an idea of just how powerful God's Word can be in directing lives, consider the story of the English ship, the *Bounty*. Captained by Lieutenant William Bligh, in 1787 it was on its way to the South Pacific to collect plants to bring back to the UK. Sailors had gladly signed up for the trip because they saw it as a trip to paradise. And sure enough, the *Bounty* stayed in Tahiti for 6 months and the sailors, led by second-in-command Fletcher

Christian, enjoyed paradise to the full. When it was time to leave, some of the men even wanted to stay behind with their island girls, but this would mean deserting their ship. Three potential deserters were flogged and, not surprisingly, the mood on the ship darkened. Then, on 28 April 1789, Fletcher Christian staged the most famous mutiny in history. Bligh and his supporters were set adrift in an overloaded lifeboat (which they miraculously navigated 3,700 miles to Timor).

The mutineers who were still aboard the *Bounty* started quarrelling about what to do next. The ship returned to Tahiti, where some of the mutineers were left, some women were kidnapped, along with a few slaves, and the ship then travelled on with the remaining crew to uninhabited Pitcairn Island, another 1,000 miles further on. There the little group distilled whisky, and drunkenness and fighting became rife in their colony. Disease and murder eventually took the lives of all the men except for one, Alexander Smith. Smith found himself the only man on the island, surrounded by women and children.

At this point an amazing change occurred. Smith discovered the ship's Bible and as he read it, he took its message to heart. He taught his fellow colonists the scriptures and helped them obey its instructions. Over the next twenty years, the message of Christ so transformed the lives of these people that, in 1808, when the ship *Topez* landed on the island, it discovered a happy society of Christians living in prosperity and peace, free from murder and crime. The Bible now remains on display in the church in Pitcairn as a monument to its transforming message.

Just as the Bible helped turn this small community around, so it can help you to find your way and discover the purpose that God has for your soul.

The Bible helps us to filter our experience

Most of us have anti-virus and firewall software on our computers so that we can avoid viruses and hackers. In other words, we filter in only what we want. Our food is printed with expiry dates to give us information about its freshness – another filter that ensures we avoid things that might be harmful to us. We even filter our water these days because we realise how much muck there is in the world today.

Do you ever feel bombarded with information and opinions? The Bible will help you to filter out what is negative, unnecessary or distracting, so that you can focus on what is right and helpful in life. In both our practical and our spiritual lives, it is essential to filter out short-term risks and long-term poisons – prevention is always better than cure. In the same way, we also need to filter out ideas that might have a negative effect on our thoughts and actions, either in the short-term or over a longer period. After all, the world is not neutral – in fact, it is full of distortions. Circulating around us are more urban myths, superstitions and false beliefs than we might first realise. Consider the following statements, which were posted on the Internet, and decide whether they are true or false.

1. A penny dropped from the Empire State Building will embed itself in the pavement.
2. You can send a coconut through the mail in the US without wrapping it.
3. The bubbles in bubble-wrap (the packing material) contain a toxic gas.
4. If the entire population of China jumped up and down at the same time, the earth's orbit would be disturbed.
5. Unless marked 'dairy', fast food shakes aren't milk, but mostly carrageen gel.
6. Welding whilst wearing contact lenses will cause the lenses to stick to your eyeballs.
7. A woman was impregnated by loose sperm while swimming in a pool.
8. Koalas are always drunk from ingesting the alcohol in eucalyptus leaves.
9. A woman adopted a stray dog in Mexico and later discovered it was a sewer rat.
10. In the US, highway workers blew up a whale and showered the town with whale blubber.
11. Some mothers like to eat the placenta of their babies, at birth.
12. A mime artist had a heart attack during his act. The audience thought it was part of the act and did nothing.
13. Bubblegum is made with spider eggs.
14. You can tell if a big operation is under way at the White House by the level of pizza orders that come from there.

Only numbers 2, 5, 10 and 11 are true. The rest are myths – false notions that come and go with

> *The Word of God has survived for thousands of years.*

time. Sometimes things that sound true prove to be nothing more than myths. Other things seem hard to believe, but are absolutely true. And many times, there is no way of knowing which is which. The truth, on the other hand, embodied in the Bible, endures forever. That explains why the Word of God has survived for thousands of years. The Bible provides us with a benchmark of truth that we can measure everything else against.

The Bible helps us to fix our course

As Christians we may well encounter negativity about our faith on a day-to-day basis – and this often comes most vehemently from friends, family and colleagues. And there is a consistent attack in the media on Christian values. Without foundations fixed in place, we can easily drift off our original course.

The Bible gives us an anchor – a sense of stability. Isaiah 8:20 says: 'Look to God's instructions and teachings! People who contradict his word are completely in the dark.' Reading the scriptures can help us to stay firm as the turbulent and corrosive sea of modern beliefs swirls around us.

The Bible will feed your soul

Psalm 119:103 says: 'How sweet your words taste to me; they are sweeter than honey.' The Bible nourishes our hungry souls – this book is soul food.

Jesus indicated that he knew this to be true when he was faced with the devil's temptations in the desert. The devil said to Jesus: '"If you are the Son of God, tell these stones to become loaves of bread." But Jesus told him, "No! The Scriptures say, 'People do not live by bread alone'"' (Matthew 4:3–5). Just as we need to feed our bodies food in order to be physically healthy, so we need to feed our souls with the truth and goodness of God's Word if we are also to be healthy in our spiritual lives.

Notice too that Jesus described himself as the bread of life: 'I am the living bread that came down from heaven. Anyone who eats this bread will live forever; and this bread, which I will offer so the world may live, is my flesh' (John 6:51). In this way, he claimed that he himself was the living fulfilment of Old Testament truth. Jesus is the living Word of

> 'I am the living bread that came down from heaven. Anyone who eats this bread will live forever; and this bread, which I will offer so the world may live, is my flesh.'

God, and is described as such in the first verses of John's Gospel: 'In the beginning the Word already existed. The Word was with God, and the Word was God. He existed in the beginning with God. God created everything through him, and nothing was created except through him. The Word gave life to everything that was created, and his life brought light to everyone' (John 1:1–4). If you have recently begun a relationship with Jesus, get to know him through reading his Word and through doing so you will nourish your soul.

These four roles of the Bible are important to us at any stage of life, but especially when we are young and facing many decisions and opportunities. On an ongoing basis, the Bible will help us to find, filter and fix things in our lives – and feed our souls at the very deepest level.

Reading Your Bible in Practice

Recently, a friend of mine came across an eighteenth-century Bible in a jumble sale. It is huge, lavishly decorated and hand printed – she felt daunted to open it and start reading! You might feel like that about your Bible – it certainly doesn't look like your average novel. And some versions are difficult to read either because of the small typeface or the old-fashioned language. However, the Bible is a book worth persisting with. George Müller, who was known for his strong faith, confided: 'The first three years after conversion, I neglected the Word of God. Since I began to search it diligently, the blessing has been wonderful. I have read the Bible through 100 times and always with increasing delight!'

The Problem of Quantity

If we spent fifteen minutes a day reading the Bible we would get through the entire book in a year. Do it the second year and the third, and then it gets familiar. Are you too busy to spend fifteen minutes a day reading God's manual for life?

Practical Tips for Bible Reading

You may want to consider a variety of approaches in starting to read the Bible. Here are a few suggestions.

- Start by reading one of the Gospels (Matthew, Mark, Luke or John). These books tell the intriguing story of the life of Jesus, and are written in very digestible language. It won't take you long to whip through one.
- Vary your reading by starting at the beginning of the Old Testament and the beginning of the New Testament. Gradually work your way through each section, reading each one each day for as long as you feel comfortable. If you decide to approach Bible reading this way, make sure you allow enough time each day for reading the New Testament – which you may find much easier to read than the Old.
- Join a Bible study group. Most churches run groups held at people's homes. There are often groups for different ages and types of people – so hopefully in your church, there'll be one that is just right for you. Each week you will study and discuss a particular passage from the Bible.
- Follow any reading guides in your Bible and explore your Bible as you would any other book – your particular version may have something unique to offer. For example, the *Life Application Study Bible* includes references to help you understand the harmony of the Gospels, the messianic prophecies and their fulfilment, as well as a 365-day reading plan.

- Use daily Bible reading notes. Many are available, either directly from churches (who often give them away free, or sell them in their bookshops) or from Christian bookshops. Each day of the year there will be a suggested Bible reading (or a few separate readings, following a theme) and questions for contemplation and prayer. For more information on Bible reading notes, see Appendix B at the end of the book.

The Problem of Choice

> *Whichever way you approach your Bible reading, make sure you own a Bible that you are comfortable with.*

Whichever way you approach your Bible reading, make sure you own a Bible that you are comfortable with. There are numerous versions available. There are Bibles for men, Bibles for women, Bibles for teenagers and Bibles that have Jesus' words in red type. There are study Bibles, electronic Bibles or CD-ROMs and of course there are also concordances and websites to help you check out words or themes. Explore your local Christian bookshop or a book-selling website to find one that feels right for you. For further advice on selecting a Bible, see Appendix A at the end of the book.

Study, Learn and Think!

In his letters, Paul urges Christians that in order to reach maturity of faith, they must continue to learn about the truth and so increase in their knowledge of God. Ephesians 4:21,22 says: 'Since you have heard about Jesus and have learned the truth that comes from him, throw off your old sinful nature and your former way of life'.

In order to grow spiritual-ly, we need to keep delving deeper into the Word of God. A great way to do this is to start reading books that unpack the Bible and bring it alive for us in our world today. I

> *In order to grow spiritually, we need to keep delving deeper into the Word of God.*

learn so much from reading about other Christians' experiences of life and God. You will have already noticed that at the end of each chapter I have suggested a few books relating to the particular theme of the chapter. Buy one or two on topics that really grab you, and keep on growing in your knowledge of the truth.

Selective Bible Reading

Sometimes, we can develop a selective mentality towards the Bible. Just as we exercise our freedom of choice in other areas of life, we can pick out what we want from the spiritual books available, can't we? We decide to absorb the bits of the Bible that suit us, and perhaps weave its wisdom into what we read elsewhere. But in order to be spiritually healthy as Christians, we need everything this book has to offer. No other wisdom or philosophy matches its brilliance and we can't accept its message in part.

A Final Word on the Problem of Context

It hurtled down the lane, hitting the pins and the result was a strike.

What do you think this phrase describes? Select one from the following possibilities:

1. An accident in a needlework factory, which led to industrial action.
2. Police strike a criminal gang by placing tacks in the road.
3. A successful experience at a local bowling alley.

Despite what our society tells us, truth is not relative (if truth was relative then that very statement would not be true!). The above phrase, whilst true to its writer, can be interpreted in different ways because we have taken it out of its original context. The writer intended to describe a successful experience at the bowling alley – the other two suggestions might be amusing but they don't reflect the author's intention. When we read the Bible we need to engage with the historical and sociological background of the part we are reading. We also need to consider the text that comes before and after the few words or verse(s) we are reading – which might considerably affect its meaning.

Consider, for a minute, the issue of slavery. The Bible contains numerous references to this issue in a way that may initially seem highly politically incorrect (in Exodus, Leviticus, Deuteronomy, Ephesians, Colossians and Philemon). This is because the word 'slave' conjures up a political scenario of which we are rightly ashamed. However, many of us quite happily employ people to work for us both as and when needed or on an ongoing basis. We have cleaners, gardeners and PAs to help us with our work.

When we read about slavery in the Bible, we are in fact reading about employees within the particular cultural and social context of the time in which it was written – when property and individual freedoms were viewed very differently than they are today. It was common for slaves to be 'bought' for a fixed number of years in Old Testament times and although we might initially be inclined to view this very negatively, we might also remember our current-day problem with short-term contracts and job insecurity. Taking on permanent slaves on a racist and abusive basis is certainly not advocated or endorsed by the Bible.

> *Taking on permanent slaves on a racist and abusive basis is certainly not advocated or endorsed by the Bible.*

If we are to truly understand the meaning of the Bible, including those sections that are hard to make sense of in our world, then we need to learn about the way people lived during the times that the Bible was written. We even need to learn about how individual words were used and the more general manner in which people normally communicated in those times.

You can see it is not always an easy matter to decide how biblical texts can be translated into real-life situations today. This is why it is helpful to study the Bible with a group of other believers and to use guides or reference books providing timelines or an historical overview. But be encouraged – this book has stood the test of time. Generation after generation of Christians have found it to be true.

The Challenge

The Bible says: 'Let the message about Christ, in all its richness, fill your lives' (Colossians 3:16). It is through reading the Bible that we will really get to grips with the message of Jesus and find out how to apply it in our lives. Just like top-class athletes, if we want to excel, we have to train hard. The more you put in, the more you get out. And the more you exercise your mind, the more efficient it will be. As you read and apply what you learn in the Bible, you will find your faith will increase and you will grow stronger spiritually.

Why not start reading the Bible today? Don't give it the dregs of your day – read it when you are feeling at your best, so that you can really focus on the meaning of the Word of God. Who knows where it might lead?

To get you started, here are some verses written by the psalmist, David. In this piece of prose, he expresses the importance of the Bible in his life.

Your word is a lamp to guide my feet
  and a light for my path.
I've promised it once, and I'll promise it again:
  I will obey your righteous regulations.
I have suffered much, O LORD;
  restore my life again as you promised.
LORD, accept my offering of praise,
  and teach me your regulations.
My life constantly hangs in the balance,
  but I will not stop obeying your instructions.
The wicked have set their traps for me,
  but I will not turn from your commandments.
Your laws are my treasure;
  they are my heart's delight.
I am determined to keep your decrees
  to the very end.
You are my refuge and my shield;
  your word is my source of hope.
(Psalm 119:105–112,114)

Prayer

'Thank you Father God for giving us your Word. Thank you Jesus for embodying the Word of God and bringing it to life. Thank you Holy Spirit that you are helping me to see the relevance of the Bible to my life today. Help me to get into this incredible book of truth and give it a place of priority in my life. Amen.'

Further Reading

The Potted Guide to Theology, Tony Gray and Steve English, Paternoster Press, 2007
Why Trust the Bible? Amy Orr-Ewing, Inter-Varsity Press, 2005

4

Prayer

The Need for Prayer

> *'Seven days
> without prayer
> makes one weak.'*

There is an old phrase about prayer that still rings true today: 'Seven days without prayer makes one weak.' While it is vital to read God's message communicated to us through the Bible, it is also necessary to talk with God. The Bible deals with a whole range of issues and can help to ground us in a Christian lifestyle, but prayer deals with the details.

Prayer has been described as the Christian's vital breath because it is the oxygen of the Christian lifestyle. Just as we die in physical terms if we don't breathe in enough oxygen, we are also in danger of dying spiritually if we neglect our need to pray. On the other hand, our effectiveness grows as we recognise our dependence on God, personally engaging with him on a daily basis.

In 1972, Jim Cymbala was asked to help pastor a small church called Brooklyn Tabernacle in a dilapidated building in New York City. The location was bad, the facilities were falling apart and only a few people attended. As Jim prayed one day about what to do, he sensed God speaking: 'If you and your wife will lead my people to pray and call upon my name, you will never lack for something fresh to preach. I will supply all the money that is needed, both for the church and for your family, and you will never have a building large enough to contain the crowds I will send in response.'

Jim went back to the church and told them that from that moment on the health of the church would be measured by its Tuesday night prayer meeting. On the first night only fifteen people came but soon – as they continued to pray – the church grew bigger. Three times they were forced to seek larger facilities and by 1985 they had 1,600 people for their Sunday service. Hundreds came to the Tuesday night prayer meeting and God brought about miraculous conversions.

Today, Brooklyn Tabernacle has 10,000 members. Besides the Tuesday meeting, there is a prayer ministry in which each hour of each day of the week, someone is praying for the church and for the lost. Lives continue to be dramatically transformed by the power of God . . . all thanks to prayer.

The nineteenth century evangelist D.L. Moody once wrote: 'Every work of God can be traced to some kneeling form.' The story of Jim Cymbala shows that these words hold as much truth today as when they were first written.

Anyone Can Pray

Now you may think you are in a different league to this praying pastor – a lower one. What if you are not good enough to meet with God in prayer?

Did you know that most of the Bible was written by three people who had committed murder? Moses, David and Paul were all guilty of murder, but because all three of them were repentant, God forgave them and used their lives in amazing ways. Praying for forgiveness enabled them to be transformed. This shouldn't come as a surprise because we are assured in 2 Chronicles 7:14: 'If my people who are called by my name will humble themselves, and pray and seek my face, and turn from their wicked ways, then I will hear from heaven, and will forgive their sins and restore their land.'

There are no leagues with God: every one of us is in the lowest league possible in comparison to the perfection of Jesus. But anyone who accepts his death for them is instantly moved up to the highest league – when God looks on those who have accepted Christ he sees the perfection of his Son in them. If we accept Jesus' forgiveness, we have direct access to God – and complete assurance that he will hear and respond to our prayers.

> *If we accept Jesus' forgiveness, we have direct access to God.*

An Open Line

Recently, I was in London and one of the places I had to go to was Lambeth Palace. I got a cab and as soon as I said, 'Lambeth Palace, please,' the driver said, 'So are you one of them, then?'

'One of what?' I asked.

'A minister . . .'

'Well, yes I am. I'm a specialist.'

Then the taxi driver said, 'Send one up for me.'

I said, 'Send one up for yourself!' He stopped the cab and looked at me.

'Send one up for me,' he said again.

'Send one up for yourself!'

He stammered, 'Oh, I, I, I didn't know people like me could.'

I said, 'Well, you can.'

'Well, how do I know he's gonna hear me?'

I said, 'Look, what's your problem? You got any problems?' He told me that he was ill, so I said, 'OK. You send one up for yourself, I'll send one up for you . . . and we will see if you get well.'

He agreed to try.

Then he said, 'Alright, then. So what do I have to do?'

I said, 'You say, "God I'm sick. Make me well."'

'What, just like that?' He was still confused so I got him to repeat it after me: 'God, I'm sick. Make me well.'

Then I said: 'OK, now I'll say my one. God, he is sick. Make him well.'

He said, 'What was that?'

'What was what?' I asked

'What is this thing I'm feeling?

'That is God's Holy Spirit.'

Then we carried on talking. He couldn't believe that God had answered his prayer – that God would do something in his life.

Why don't you say a prayer for yourself too? You could say: 'God, I want you to do in my life what you have done in other people's lives.' Don't worry about the language you use, just talk to God naturally, as you would to any friend. If you need a miracle, ask for one.

Who are You Developing a Relationship With?

If you said a prayer just now, you took a step that will have brought you into closer relationship with God. Hang on a minute, though: how much thought have you given to the kind of God that you are developing a relationship with?

God's key characteristics are as follows: he is all-loving, totally powerful (omnipotent), present everywhere (omnipresent), all-knowing (omniscient), eternal and holy. God is not merely a force or a power – he is a personal God who we can talk to. God has emotions of care and even anger. This all means he is a God we can relate to because we are a bit like him.

In 1 John 4, God is described as being love. In 1 Corinthians 13, Paul gives an explanation of the nature of love. As you read it, remember that this is a description of the nature of God:

> Love is patient and kind. Love is not jealous or boastful or proud or rude. It does not demand its own way. It is not irritable, and it keeps no record of being wronged. It does not rejoice about injustice but rejoices whenever the truth wins out. Love never gives up, never loses faith, is

always hopeful, and endures through every circumstance. Prophecy and speaking in unknown languages and special knowledge will become useless. But love will last forever! (1 Corinthians 13:4–8)

As you start to pray, you will begin to discover more of God's good, loving character. Imagine for a moment that you are introduced to someone new and you soon become friends with them. You meet up and chat regularly. Even though you are in regular contact with this person, there may still be enormous areas of their life that you do not know about. As the friendship develops, the gaps in your knowledge slowly decrease. It is possible that several months into the friendship you stumble across things that really surprise you: your new buddy turns out to be fluent in Greek and into cycling. As you get to know her, you adjust your opinions and your friendship adapts to these new facts. So it is with God: we always go on learning about him. (God certainly is fluent in Greek but he probably doesn't spend his time cycling!) What we find out about God's character encourages us to keep exploring him through prayer.

> *As you start to pray, you will begin to discover more of God's good, loving character.*

How Does a Relationship with God Work in Practice?

Jesus showed us how an intimate, respectful relationship with God can work day to day. Firstly, he suggested we call God 'Abba', which is the intimate but respectful word 'Daddy' in Aramaic, the language Jesus grew up speaking. And Jesus also demonstrated talking with God as if to a loving father. Both his instructions and his example show us that our relationship with God is to be personal, practical and two-way. Given that we are talking here about communicating with the all-powerful being who gave us life, this really is an awesome concept – and it is only thanks to Jesus' death that this relationship is possible. (Before he came along, only the highest Jewish priest had access to God, in the holiest area of their temple. At the moment that Jesus died, though, the curtain to this area ripped in two. See Matthew 27:45–54 for the full account.) But don't be overawed or ashamed, however mind-blowing this is. The God that Jesus made it possible for us to love, talk to and listen to, accepts us just as we are.

God Listens and Speaks

Mark Twain once said: 'I don't know of a single foreign product that enters this country untaxed, except the answer to prayer.' Expect God to respond to your prayers – he hears every one of them. Our God is a God who came to earth as a man so as to interact up close and personal with humanity, and he still likes to do so today. Speak to him and ask him to speak to you, and he will do! When William Temple was the Archbishop of Canterbury he said: 'When we pray coincidences happen. When we don't, they don't.' Spend some time asking

Christians to tell you about prayers that God has answered for them. I can guarantee you will hear some incredible stories.

But remember, too, that not all our prayers will be answered. God knows what is best for us and he doesn't always answer our prayers in the way we expect. Sometimes he says, 'Yes,' sometimes 'No,' and sometimes the answer is: 'Wait!' Many centuries ago, an unnamed nun said a very useful prayer: 'Dear God, please give me the courage to change the things I can change, the maturity to leave what I can't and the wisdom to know the difference.' A key part of our journey towards God in prayer is learning to trust that he knows best, and is still intervening in our lives even when this is hard to see or understand.

> *But remember, too, that not all our prayers will be answered.*

Jesus' Prayer Life

There are frequent references to Jesus' approach to prayer throughout the Gospels. He prayed in a variety of ways, knowing that it was vital to spend time with his heavenly father, and to hear what his father was saying to him. As followers of Jesus, we need to follow the example he set. Why and when did he pray?

- He prayed to his father, who he was close to. Sometimes quite spontaneously he thanked God for something, e.g. in Matthew 11:25. In John 17, Jesus talked intimately to God about what he knew was going to happen.

- He prayed first thing in the morning. See Mark 1:35 for an example of how he got up before daybreak to pray.
- He prayed to prepare himself for something. The evening before he chose his twelve disciples, Jesus climbed a mountain to pray for the whole night (see Luke 6:12,13). Just before he was arrested, Jesus withdrew to an olive grove to pray with his closest disciples (see Matthew 26:36–39). There he prayed for God's will, not his own, to be done during the next few hours and days.
- He prayed when he was tired or after he had done some amazing things. In Luke 5:12–16, we learn that Jesus healed a man with an advanced case of leprosy. (Not surprisingly, this caused his popularity to rise, even though he asked the man not to tell anyone about the miracle!) We are told that after healing people, Jesus often went into the wilderness to pray. After making enough food to feed 5,000 out of just a little bread and fish, he also withdrew to pray, again taking some of his close disciples with him (see Luke 9:10–17).
- He prayed for people, so as to bless them. In Matthew 19:13–15 it is recorded that Jesus agreed to pray over some children who had been brought to him, placing his hands on their heads as he blessed them.

The Jesus Prayer

As well as modelling our prayer life on that of Jesus, we can also learn from the teaching he gave on this topic. In fact, Jesus taught us only one prayer, which in one translation is only 63 words long. Through his words, which make up what we know as 'The Lord's Prayer', we learn about God's priorities:

'Our Father in heaven,
May your name be kept holy,
May your Kingdom come soon,
May your will be done on earth, as it is in heaven.
Give us today the food we need,
And forgive us our sins, as we have forgiven those who
  sin against us.
And don't let us yield to temptation,
But rescue us from the evil one.'
(Matthew 6:9–13)

Since this is such an important prayer and it comes directly from Jesus, here it is in two other translations . . .

First, here it is as it appears in *The Message*:

> *This is such an important prayer and it comes directly from Jesus.*

Our Father in heaven,
Reveal who you are.
Set the world right;
Do what's best – as above, so below.
Keep us alive with three square meals.
Keep us forgiven with you and forgiving others.
Keep us safe from ourselves and the Devil.

You are in charge!
You can do anything you want!
You are ablaze in beauty!
Yes. Yes. Yes.

Here it is as translated in *The Street Bible*:

God in heaven, you are our dad.
We respect everything you stand for. We want others
  to.
Please bring heaven on earth: people living life your
  way, like the angels do.
Please bring us what we need to keep us going each
  day.
Please acquit us, as we cancel our grievances and
  throw them all away.
Please pull us back from the edge of evil, if we are
  falling, or being thrown.
'Cos you are all that matters; you are able to do it
  and you are to take the credit.
You are on your own.
It is your throne.
Absolutely!

At Princess Diana's funeral, an estimated 1.2 billion people prayed this prayer during the service. But how many of those people actually believed what they were saying, were ready to take action or were willing to align their attitudes with their prayer? It is one thing to say, 'Forgive us our sins as we forgive those who sin against us', but are we willing to actually do it?

What to Pray About

The Lord's Prayer is a useful template for our prayers. It shows that we can thank God, give him glory, ask him to provide for us, forgive us, protect us, reveal himself to us, and keep us on the straight and narrow. From it we can deduce five broad guidelines for what to pray about.

1. Pray your thoughts and feelings to God

You can find examples of heartfelt prayers, in which feelings are expressed to God, in Psalm 23 and in Luke 2:29–32.

Feel free to chat to God. In John 15:15 Jesus says: 'I no longer call you slaves, because a master doesn't confide in his slaves. Now you are my friends, since I have told you everything the Father told me.' Think of prayer as time with your friend Jesus – you can be as natural with him as you would any other friend. Whatever we are thinking or worrying about we can bring to God in prayer: it all matters to him. In other words, we need to change our matters of care into matters of prayer. Talk to God about the people and things you care most about and you will soon find that life's best outlook is a prayerful up-look!

2. Pray to ask forgiveness

This is best expressed in The Lord's Prayer but see also Psalm 25.

Imagine that you have a bow and arrow, and are about to shoot at a target. You put the arrow in the bow, pull it back and fire. It doesn't hit the target. God's target is very simple – it only has two circles. The inner one says 'Love God', the outer one says 'Love your neighbour'. Every day you and I have

> *Through his Word,
> and his Spirit
> working in your
> conscience, you
> will hear him
> gently letting you
> know.*

a new bow of opportunity and we frequently fail to reach the target. Each day, ask God to show you where you have missed the target recently. Through his Word, and his Spirit working in your conscience, you will hear him gently letting you know. Simply ask his forgiveness for your mistakes (the Christian word for this is 'confession'), accept his forgiveness and ask for help in hitting the target in the future. In Luke 22:39,40 (as well as in The Lord's Prayer) Jesus advised his disciples to pray that they would not give in to temptation. You can pray that, too.

3. Pray to ask God for help

In Acts 1:24–26, the apostles pray to know how to make a decision, just as a servant did many hundreds of years before in Genesis 24:12–14.

You can ask God to provide you with opportunities or material needs, to help you with decisions or with your relationships with others. When you do ask for help or provision, be clear about the details. Although God already knows all that goes on in our lives, if we are to develop a relationship with him we need to depend on him through prayer. See Acts 4:24–30 for an example of a prayer with a request, which also includes lots of details!

Let's remember though, that while God cares about our bodies and our needs and we can pray for these, often what we want and what we need are quite different.

Did you know that the average family ambition is to make as much money as they are spending? The multimillionaire John D. Rockefeller was asked, 'How much money does it take a person to be really satisfied?' He answered: 'Just a little bit more.' But the truth is that we find contentment when we desire less not more. Miraculously, as we seek God in prayer, we find that our prayers become less selfish. We find ourselves praying less for material things that are 'wants' rather than 'needs', and gradually we are able to discern the difference. So we should pray like this: 'Allow us to have what we need.' Ask Jesus to help you turn away from your false idols, whether they are money, clothes, drink, sex or anything else.

Whatever you are thinking or feeling right now, whatever your wants and needs, another useful little prayer is to ask that you will go up a gear and not cruise along in neutral.

4. Pray for others

We can see examples of this in Numbers 6:24–26, Exodus 32:11–13 and Jude 24.

As well as being realistic and humble about our own needs, let's remember the needs of others. Christians call this 'intercession'. Pray for your family and other people you know, and for everyone who has recently started following Jesus or who has recommitted their lives to him. Pray that churches will continue to have the right focus and be full of enthusiasm so that others may share the joy of forgiveness and transformation in the Holy Spirit. Pray for the needs of people suffering all around the world. And pray for anybody you know who has not yet come to understand the message of Jesus.

5. Pray to say thank you

Have a look at 1 Chronicles 29:10–13 and Psalm 105:1–7. In the New Testament, Mary prayed a similar prayer of praise after her cousin Elizabeth recognised that Mary was going to give birth to the Lord, Jesus Christ (see Luke 1:46–55).

Last but not least, let's show our great God some appreciation! A lot of people give thanks and praise to God when they go to church, but you can do this on your own any time. In 1 Thessalonians 5:17,18 Paul writes: 'Never stop praying. Be thankful in all circumstances, for this is God's will for you who belong to Christ Jesus.' Try reading a psalm aloud to God as a prayer of thanks, or listen to some worship music and echo the words in your heart. Tell Jesus today about the things in your life that you are grateful for.

A lot of people give thanks and praise to God when they go to church, but you can do this on your own any time.

Practical Ideas for Prayer

Prayer can take a variety of forms – be creative and mix it up! Here are some ideas to get you started.

• Slowly read a Bible verse several times, thinking about the meaning of each word. As you reflect on it, let the verse inspire you in prayer. Ask God how you could live out that verse today and pray for the strength to do so. This is a meditative way of praying.

- Buy a journal. Use it as you would a diary, but add in prayers for yourself, others and special Bible verses. Before long you will start to be able to look back and see that God is answering your prayers.
- Go on prayer walks. Being surrounded by the beauty of creation often inspires us to look towards God and helps us to feel close to him.
- Listen to worship music and allow this to inspire you in prayer. Think about your postures in prayer too: try lying down, standing up or kneeling. Are you engaging all five of your senses as you pray?
- For a healthy prayer life, learn to pray with others as well as alone. Find a friend at church and meet regularly to pray. Some churches will group members into 'prayer triplets' who meet to share honestly about their lives in an accountable way, and pray for each other.

> *Find a friend at church and meet regularly to pray.*

A Few Words of Warning!

Here are five things to consider as you get your prayer life on track.

1. Make time to pray

Many people worship their work, work at their play and play at their worship. Consider giving the first part of every day to spending time worshipping God, reading the Bible and praying. Here is a great reminder and encouragement to be anchored in God. It is a poem by Grace L. Naessens called 'No Time to Pray'.

I got up early one morning
And rushed right into the day
I had so much to accomplish
That I didn't have time to pray

Problems just tumbled about me
And heavier came each task
'Why doesn't God help me' I wondered
He answered 'You just didn't ask'

I wanted to see joy and beauty
But the day toiled on, grey and bleak
I wondered why God didn't show me
He said 'You just didn't seek'

I tried to come into God's presence
I used all my keys at the lock
God gently and lovingly chided
'My child why didn't you knock?'

I woke up early this morning
And paused before entering the day
I had so much to accomplish
That I had to take time to pray

2. Don't be ostentatious!

In Luke 18:10–14 we learn that Jesus reminded people not to use prayer as an excuse to show off. Here is the story in full:

> 'Two men went to the Temple to pray. One was a Pharisee, and the other was a despised tax collector. The Pharisee stood by himself and prayed this prayer: "I thank you, God, that I am not a sinner like everyone else. For I don't cheat, I don't sin, and I don't commit adultery. I'm certainly not like that tax collector! I fast twice a week, and I give you a tenth of my income."
>
> 'But the tax collector stood at a distance and dared not even lift his eyes to heaven as he prayed. Instead, he beat his chest in sorrow, saying, "O God, be merciful to me, for I am a sinner." I tell you, this sinner, not the Pharisee, returned home justified before God. For those who exalt themselves will be humbled, and those who humble themselves will be exalted.'

It seems we have got to watch our attitude! It is not that surprising, considering the all-knowing God knows what we really mean and think anyway.

3. Be sincere

As well as praying specifically, we also need to pray sincerely. For example, at mealtimes have you ever thought about the way some people say grace? You look down at the meal

> *As well as praying specifically, we also need to pray sincerely.*

and see a nutritional nightmare – grease bubbling, salt glistening, a sugary drink on the side. But still you hear your host say, 'Bless this food and may it make us healthy.' I'm not sure we should ask God to bless junk food and expect him to miraculously transform it so that it has nutritional value! Doing that is acting like the 12-year-old who after taking a geography test prayed, 'Dear God, please make Glasgow the capital of Scotland.' We need to be realistic and sincere in our demands, doing as much as we humanly can to assist God along the way, while remembering that miracles are possible.

4. *Be persistent*

In Luke 18:1–8, we read the following account:

> One day Jesus told his disciples a story to show that they should always pray and never give up. 'There was a judge in a certain city,' he said, 'who neither feared God nor cared about people. A widow of that city came to him repeatedly, saying, "Give me justice in this dispute with my enemy." The judge ignored her for a while, but finally he said to himself, "I don't fear God or care about people, but this woman is driving me crazy. I'm going to see that she gets justice, because she is wearing me out with her constant requests!"'
>
> Then the Lord said, 'Learn a lesson from this unjust judge. Even he rendered a just decision in the end. So don't you think God will surely give justice to his chosen people who cry out to him day and night? Will he keep putting them off? I tell you, he will grant justice to them quickly!'

The message is simple: don't give up! George Müller (a nineteenth century evangelist) helped 100,000 orphans in his life. He also understood the need for persistence in prayer and prayed for five of his friends who were not Christians. It took 5 years for the first one to be converted, 10 years for the second one, 25 years for the third one and 50 years for the fourth one to be converted. And what about the fifth one? 52 years after Müller started praying for him he converted – at Müller's funeral.

5. *Use the word 'amen' wisely*

'Amen' is a most remarkable word. It was trans-literated directly from the Hebrew into the Koine Greek of the New Testament, then into Latin and into English and many other languages. It has been called the best-known word in human speech. It basically means 'be true' and was the word that Jews used to confirm or agree with something, whether it was a prayer or a blessing. In modern English speech, it means 'so be it', 'let it be so' or even 'let what we have said be binding on us'.

So by using the word 'amen' at the end of a prayer, Jews of Jesus' day would have been making that prayer their own – and that is what you will be doing too if you use it yourself. By saying the word 'amen' you will be saying: 'I personally approve of and agree with what has just been said. I allow myself to be bound by its terms.' So it is like adding a verbal signature to anything that has just been prayed!

There was once a church with a small but vocal 'Amen Corner'. Especially vocal was Deacon Jones, who led the 'Amen Corner'. One day when Preacher Brown began his sermon with the words, 'Let the church walk,' Deacon Jones shouted in response, 'Amen! Let the church walk!'

Preacher Brown continued, 'Let the church run!' and Deacon Jones followed along with, 'Amen! Let the church run!'

Preacher Brown got even more excited and exclaimed, 'Let the church fly!'

And Deacon Jones almost jumped out of his pew shouting, 'Amen! Let the church fly!'

Then Preacher Brown looked at them earnestly and said, 'And if the church is going to fly, it will take money!' Whereupon Deacon Jones replied, 'Let the church walk!'

> *Next time you say a prayer, don't just say 'amen' out of habit.*

Next time you say a prayer, don't just say 'amen' out of habit. Pause and ask yourself some questions: am I prepared to commit myself to what I have prayed? Am I prepared to live in a way that is consistent with my prayer? Am I prepared for God to answer my prayers? If you are, then go ahead and say 'amen' with faith, confidence and expectation.

Christ is Praying for You

As you start to develop your prayer life, be reassured not only that other Christians will be praying for you (they will) but also that Jesus is praying for you, too. After all, he is our advocate in heaven before God, so long as we remain faithful to him. As Robert Murray M'Cheyne, a nineteenth century pastor from Dundee, once said: 'If I could hear Christ praying for me in the next room, I would not fear a million enemies. Yet distance makes no difference. He is praying for me.'

Transformed Through Prayer

Prayer can be a real challenge, even for the most mature Christian. And when our will resists God's, it seems even harder to spend lots of time talking to him! I regularly pray a prayer that goes like this: 'God, I want to want what you want me to want! Would you gently mould my heart and desires so that my priorities and prayers are aligned with your will? Amen.'

Romans 12:2 says: 'Don't copy the behaviour and customs of this world, but let God transform you into a new person by changing the way you think. Then you will learn to know God's will for you, which is good and pleasing and perfect.' As we mature in faith and become more like God, we will increasingly know his will and pray in line with it. As this happens, we see more prayers answered. A wise man once said, 'To pray is to change.' Prayer is an essential part of the exciting miracle of our transformation.

Prayer

This prayer was one of Jesus' disciples' requests (see Luke 11:1). I love its simplicity:

Lord, teach us to pray.

Further Reading

What You Always Wanted to Know About Prayer . . . But Were Afraid to Ask, Ian Coffey, CWR, 2007

24–7 Prayer Manual, Pete Greig, Kingsway Publications, 2003
A Celebration of Discipline: The Path to Spiritual Growth, Richard J. Foster, Hodder & Stoughton Religious, 1998
God's Priorities, J.John, Kingsway Publications, 2001

5

Church

I Have to go *Where?*

It may not come as a surprise to hear that you need to go to church if you are a Christian. However, you may end up being surprised at what you find there. Church is much more than a building – it is a community, or family of believers. So if you have already begun to follow Jesus, you are already part of the church. Church buildings are simply places where other members of God's family hang out together.

Church is Essential for Your Spiritual Health

You might have previously thought of church as a cold, lifeless place where a few people stand up, sit down and weakly sing a few hymns. But let me tell you this: people who go to church are part of a revolutionary crowd. They

> *People who go to church are part of a revolutionary crowd.*

know that being a Christian is not easy. And they have also worked out that going to church helps to ensure the survival of your faith.

The letter that was written to the Hebrew church (a group of Christians who were probably second generation Jews) says: 'Let us think of ways to motivate one another to acts of love and good works. And let us not neglect our meeting together, as some people do, but encourage one another' (Hebrews 10:24,25). St Augustine said, 'You cannot have God as your father, without having the church as your mother.' Church is essential to remaining strong in your faith.

Let's take a closer look at some of the benefits to getting involved in church.

1. You will be able to worship God

In church you will meet with a group of people who also want to live lives that bring worship to our creator. And so time is set aside in church to give expression to the joy and thankfulness in our hearts. In his book *It's Not About Me* (Thomas Nelson, 2004), Max Lucado expresses beautifully what it means to worship God. He quotes Romans 11:36: 'For everything comes from him and exists by his power and is intended for his glory. All glory to him forever!' and then 1 Corinthians 8:6a 'But we know that there is only one God, the Father, who created everything, and we live for him.' Lucado then writes:

Why does the earth spin? For him.
Why do you have talents and abilities? For him.

Why do you have money or poverty? For him.
Strengths or struggles? For him.
Everything and everyone exists to reveal his glory.
Including you.

We will return to the practicalities of worshipping in church later in this chapter.

2. *You will make friends*

At church you will meet other Christians, reminding you that you don't have to face life's challenges alone. Belonging to a church, and particularly a small group within it, will bring you into regular contact with people who will encourage you in your faith – and you will be able to encourage them, too. The Christian word used to express this is 'fellowship'. When Paul wrote to the Christians in Rome, after asking them to pray for his safety, he said: 'Then, by the will of God, I will be able to come to you with a joyful heart, and we will be an encouragement to each other' (Romans 15:32). Being church is about being on the same team. People will ask you how it is going, and when things aren't going too well, they will be rooting for you. None of us were made to take this journey alone.

3. *You will be able to pray with friends*

We learn from the New Testament that prayer is a vital component of church. In Acts 12:5 we read: 'while Peter was in prison, the church prayed very earnestly for him.' Most churches encourage their members to pray both during services and in smaller groups.

4. You will learn

In church you will receive biblical teaching to stimulate your mind, inspire and nourish you. Through

> *In church you will receive biblical teaching to stimulate your mind, inspire and nourish you.*

it you will be refreshed and renewed, enabling you to persevere in your journey as a Christian. Church is a time set aside each week to meet with and listen to God's truth as a community. Although God is with us all the time, in church you will often find

that you experience a more powerful sense of his presence.

5. You will find ways of serving in God's kingdom

You can start putting your faith into action at church. You could offer to help out with Sunday school, a youth group, serving coffee (which my wife Killy and I did once a month for 3 years) or blessing those in need in another creative way. Simply spending time talking to someone at church who rarely has the opportunity for a caring, friendly chat could bless them enormously. Somehow, in time, you will find ways to contribute to your church family.

God has given gifts to each of us; serving at church is a great way to start using them to glorify him. In Ephesians 4:11–13 we read:

> Now these are the gifts Christ gave to the church: the apostles, the prophets, the evangelists, and the pastors and teachers. Their responsibility is to equip God's

people to do his work and build up the church, the body of Christ. This will continue until we all come to such unity in our faith and knowledge of God's Son that we will be mature in the Lord, measuring up to the full and complete standard of Christ.

6. You will join a team with the potential to change the world

How often do you see a really diverse group of people – of all ages, races, sexes and backgrounds come together in a unified way? Not very often! The Bible tells us that each one of us has been adopted by God. Whoever we are, if we follow Jesus, we have become his brothers and sisters, brought together in the family of church.

And how often do you see a big community of people living and working together effectively? Not very often! In church we care for each other, submit to one another, bother about the very weakest person in the group and carry each other in the hard times. We are not exclusive but welcome everybody in. In Ephesians 4:15,16 we read: 'Christ . . . is the head of his body, the church. He makes the whole body fit together perfectly. As each part does its own special work, it helps the other parts grow, so that the whole body is healthy and growing and full of love.'

Again in 1 Corinthians 12:14–21, Paul uses the metaphor of the human body to describe a healthy, welcoming church community in which everyone has a part to play:

The body has many different parts, not just one part. If the foot says, 'I am not a part of the body because I

am not a hand,' that does not make it any less a part
of the body. And if the ear says, 'I am not part of the
body because I am not an eye,' would that make it any
less a part of the body? If the whole body were an eye,
how would you hear? Or if your whole body were an ear,
how would you smell anything? But our bodies have many
parts, and God has put each part just where he wants
it. How strange a body would be if it had only one part!
Yes, there are many parts, but only one body. The eye
can never say to the hand, 'I don't need you.' The head
can't say to the feet, 'I don't need you.'

As we grow together as a functioning body, we
increase in potential to bless and bring God's love
to those in our local area, in our nation and even
across our world. God's church is his vehicle bringing
restoration to all people and his damaged creation.
We have the privilege of being part of that exciting
mission.

> *God's church
> is his vehicle
> bringing
> restoration to all
> people and his
> damaged creation.*

What are the Key Ingredients to Church?

There are many types of church, and you and I
might feel comfortable worshipping in very different
environments. Essentially, however, churches are
made up of the same basic ingredients: they facilitate
believers in worshipping together, encourage their
spiritual well-being and help believers to witness to
others outside the church about Jesus.

1. Worship

Confusingly, Christians use the word 'worship' in two different ways. Firstly, it is used to refer to the general content of a church service, which might include a talk or sermon, a Bible reading or discussion, some time spent singing, praying, serving or encouraging one another. All these are important ingredients in a church service.

Secondly, 'worship' is used to refer to music or singing that brings praises to God. A whole variety of approaches can be taken to sung worship. While one of your local churches may get its songs from the traditional Anglican hymn book (first published in the nineteenth century), another – just around the corner – may use a more modern songbook. If you visit a convent, such as the Community of St Mary the Virgin in Wantage, Oxfordshire, you will find nuns singing plainsong, continuing the tradition begun in the thirteenth century! If you go to a charismatic or Pentecostal church service, you may well see other people raising their arms and waving them around. You may also hear people speaking in tongues.

We can worship God in all sorts of ways. Giving money or time, serving the poor or helping at church may well be part of the way that you worship God. I recently heard of a church that hung a sign on the inside of its doors reminding people as they left the building: 'Worship starts here'. Be creative and open-minded in expressing your praise to your creator.

2. Well-being

Some churches may seem to be more 'caring' or 'pastoral' towards their congregation than others. In your local church you may find listening groups and people to pray with who will support you in your own life choices and problems. Or the system may be much more informal – with the general expectation that people will spontaneously strike up friendships and ask help from each other. In the same way, some churches will assign an experienced Christian to you, who will occasionally contact you and offer to come round for a chat (some Christians might call this person a mentor), while others will leave you to monitor your spiritual and personal well-being yourself. Think about how a formal or informal system is helpful to you in your relationship with God.

When we look for a church, we often naturally choose one attended by people in the same life stage as ourselves. But keep an open mind. If you see a mass of elderly faces, don't automatically screen people out. Just because someone is older, it doesn't necessarily mean they are not loving or welcoming! Most older people have fascinating stories to tell and a whole lifetime of experience to share, which may just come in handy if you are experiencing problems that

> *When we look for a church, we often naturally choose one attended by people in the same life stage as ourselves.*

none of your friends can help you with. Finding spiritual well-being in church does not necessarily equate to feeling comfortable all the time.

In fact, if your church does seem very 'comfortable', something might be awry. In the book *Intelligent Church* (Zondervan Publishing House, 2006), Steve Chalke and Anthony Watkis stress the importance of church being a community. Just as God is Trinitarian (three in one: Father, Son and Holy Spirit) so our church should be inherently relational. The authors write: 'If God is community, a person can never become his or her true self in isolation apart from society. Humanity is designed not only with the capacity but also the need for community. Genuine personhood is something that we can enter into only by means of relationship with others.'

The book goes on to explain that communities are of course messy! 'In many senses, the church is a hospital – it is a place of spiritual, social, emotional, moral and psychological healing. And just as in hospital, patients suffer from different conditions, are at different levels of health and are at different stages of the healing process, so it is with the church . . . No hospital is a centre of physical perfection, and neither is a church one of spiritual perfection – rather, both are messy environments full of messed-up people striving to be less so.' Seek out a messy, relational church that challenges you to keep on growing.

One more thing: don't worry about being judged! Everyone who goes to church because he or she has accepted the message Jesus brought will understand just how imperfect humans can be. People are unlikely to be shocked by your own personal dilemmas. We all face enormous temptations, doubts and worries and we all find different ways of coping. Sharing with other people will not only help you to feel better, it'll also help you to become better at following the path Jesus intended for you.

3. Witness

This word simply means sharing our faith with others through both our words and actions. Confusingly, sometimes it is also known as evangelism or mission. In his book *The Living Church* (Inter-Varsity Press, 2007), John Stott explains the importance of the church's commitment to mission:

> He calls us to enter other people's worlds, as he entered ours. All authentic mission is incarnational mission. We are called to enter other people's social and cultural reality: into their thought-world, struggling to understand their misunderstandings of the gospel, and into the pain of their alienation, weeping with those who weep. And all this without compromising our Christian beliefs, values and standards.

Despite the fact that you or I only know Jesus because someone else bothered to let us know the Good News about him, witness is an area of church life that is often neglected. We quickly become nervous about what people will think when we mention Jesus. Many new Christians avoid doing this like the plague! Who wants to look foolish talking about Jesus? Is life not difficult enough already?

In my experience, new Christians who have honestly told others about their faith from the start have often gone on to grow and mature most quickly. While we always need to be gentle, sensitive and respectful (and carefully pick our moments) in talking about Jesus, it is

> *New Christians who have honestly told others about their faith from the start have often gone on to grow and mature most quickly.*

often surprising how positively people respond to our story of discovering him. We all have a story to tell and yours may well inspire other people who are in a similar situation to you. Your being brave and open may just help someone else. As you start to put your faith into action and speak out about it, you will be reminded of just how real and life-changing Jesus is.

Remember: witnessing to Christ is not just about the words we say. Living out our faith and actively serving others displays integrity and consistency between our words and our actions. Caring for someone who is hard to love speaks volumes about the kind of God you know. As Christians, it is essential that we convey to others both verbally and visually the Good News of Jesus Christ. We will look at this in further detail in Chapter 8.

Finding a Church

One way of finding a church is to check out www.findachurch.co.uk. Simply enter in your postcode and see what comes up in your area. Since many churches are not yet listed on this website, you would also do well to do a Google search for 'church' + the name of your city, town or village. When you have found a church that appeals, simply go along for a few services. See how you feel and consider how much you are learning. Is this a place where you will be able to make friends and worship comfortably? Is this a place where you will want to come regularly? Are you being taught God's truth here?

Each church will probably have more than one service each Sunday, conducted in a different style – so it is worth exploring other services at the same church before moving on to another one! Be part of a church that is committed to worship, well-being and witness.

Give Church a Chance

A friend moved to a new city and spent three months visiting churches, trying to find the ideal one for her. She would analyse them with a critical eye, spot the faults then move on. After three months passed, she realised what an unrealistic, judgemental attitude she had developed and went back and joined the first church she had visited! No church is a perfect church, because they are full of imperfect people. Choose a church, get involved and give it a real chance before you contemplate leaving. Expect it to take several weeks, or even months, before you really feel settled and at home there.

How Am I Meant to Behave in Church?

It is easy to get the impression that on attending church we should be on our best behaviour, rather like God were some sort of headmaster in the sky whose school children gather together to impress him with their smart uniforms and good behaviour each week. In fact, it is in church that we should really get real with God, knowing that he and those around us respond with grace to our mistakes. At the same time, a church is a community of people seeking to grow in love, trust and respect for God and each other. Everyone has a part to play in making the church community a happy and holy place to be. We need to make sincere friendships there, and learn to love the members of our church family who are hard to love. The Bible gives us some good guidance in how best to do so, which we will take a look at now.

Be honest about yourself

Dr Leonard Keeler, who devised the lie detector, surveyed 25,000 people and concluded that people are basically dishonest. We live in a society of truth decay. Here are some examples to prove the point . . .

> *We live in a society of truth decay.*

A man spent a fruitless day fishing then picked out three big fish from the market. 'Before you wrap them,' he said to the fishmonger, 'toss them to me one by one. In that way I'll be able to tell my wife I caught them and be telling the truth.'

A man was arrested for stealing a car. He said he had found the car in front of a cemetery and so he assumed the owner was dead.

An advertisement for electricians with expertise in using Sontag connectors received 179 applications . . . even though there is no such thing as a 'Sontag connector'. A research organisation ran the advertisement to find out how many applicants falsify their CVs.

On a beautiful summer's day, four female students decided to go for a drive instead of showing up for a test at college. The following day, they explained to the lecturer that they had had a flat tyre. The lecturer accepted the girls' excuse, much to their relief. She simply said, 'Since you missed yesterday's test, you must take it now. Please sit in the four corners of this room without talking.' When they were seated, she said: 'On your paper, write the answer to this question: Which tyre was flat?'

What motivates us to lie? One reason is that we don't want to take responsibility for the things that we do. We are afraid of what will happen if we tell the truth. But if you speak dishonestly about your own personality, life or behaviour, it is likely to lead to a bad relationship with another person, which goes against the grain of trying to build a healthy church community.

Jesus encouraged us to examine our own hearts because 'What you say flows from what is in your heart' (Luke 6:45). Our words reveal our character; they reveal who we really are. Sometimes accepting who we really are is so painful for us that we want to deny our own failings both to others and ourselves. The church is a place where you are accepted and loved, whoever you are, whatever you have done, whatever mess you are beginning to walk away from. With time your church should become your safe haven to 'let it all hang out', have a cry and allow yourself to be the real you.

Enjoy yourself!

Traditional expressions of church have sometimes been very serious. Without delving into a series of criticisms of the way church has been done in the past, suffice it to say that church is meant to be a place where you can be real enough and feel safe enough to laugh with others, and have a really good time!

Be careful how you speak in church

Two thousand years ago, the apostle James wrote:

> If we could control our tongues, we would be perfect and could also control ourselves in every other way. We can make a large horse go wherever we want by means of a small bit in its mouth. And a small rudder makes a huge ship turn wherever the pilot chooses to go, even though the winds are strong. In the same way, the tongue is a small thing that makes grand speeches. But a tiny spark can set a great forest on fire. And the tongue is a flame of fire. It is a whole world of wickedness, corrupting your entire body. It can set your whole life on fire, for it is set on fire by hell itself.
> (James 3:2–6)

Millions of tongues have proved the truth of James' words. As we get involved in the church family, we need to learn to speak in ways that are honourable to Jesus: with honesty, kindness, gentleness and respect.

> *As we get involved in the church family, we need to learn to speak in ways that are honourable to Jesus.*

Honour other people

The sight of a battered reputation doesn't disturb some people who would faint at the sight of blood. Slander is malicious untruth with the intention of doing harm. Few of us are guilty of this, but most of us are very guilty when it comes to careless use of words which ruin another person's reputation. Take the word 'but', for example. What kind of effect does it have if we say, 'He is good but . . .' 'She is popular but . . .'? Have you ever heard someone say, 'I'd better not say anything'? The insinuation is enough to ruin the other person's reputation. Insinuation is very common today – it is one of the main tools used by spin doctors (now a feature of British politics) but even in Shakespeare's day it was well known. In the play *Othello*, a jealous husband listens to and believes slanderous rumours that his wife is having an affair. In his rage, he murders his wife, learning almost immediately afterwards that the rumours had all been lies. Make sure that you don't have someone else's unhappiness on your conscience.

Gossip

Instead of honouring other people by speaking carefully, gossip is talking freely about others, without worrying about the consequences. Let's hear it from the horse's mouth . . .

'My name is gossip. I have no respect for justice. I maim without killing. I break hearts and ruin lives. I am cunning, malicious and gather strength with age. The more I am quoted, the more I am believed. I flourish at every level of society. My victims are helpless. They cannot protect themselves against me because I have no face. To track me down is impossible. The harder you try, the more elusive I become. I am nobody's friend. Once I tarnish a reputation it is never the same. I topple governments, wreck marriages, ruin careers, cause sleepless nights and heartache. I spawn suspicion and generate grief. I make innocent people cry on their pillows. Even my name hisses. Gossssip.'

Honesty means that everything we say must be true, not that everything that is true must be said. In any community of people, there are bound to be situations in which it is appropriate to speak up with certain facts and information. If we are going to give a job reference, let's be wise and honest with what we know. The key is this: hold to the truth in love. Say what you mean, mean what you say, but don't say it mean.

Excel in encouraging others

It is often appropriate to show genuine appreciation to others – something that many of us don't do nearly enough! Try to build up others in your church,

> *It is often appropriate to show genuine appreciation to others – something that many of us don't do nearly enough!*

noticing their strengths and giving thanks to God for them as well as pointing them out. When you see someone actively serving God, give them some positive (or if appropriate, constructive) feedback. You will be amazed how much this will spur them on and build a healthy friendship between the two of you.

Don't get into disputes

Paul repeatedly emphasised in his letters that people in churches should make every effort to get along with each other. In 1 Corinthians 1:10 he says: 'I appeal to you, dear brothers and sisters, by the authority of our Lord Jesus Christ, to live in harmony with each other. Let there be no divisions in the church. Rather, be of one mind, united in thought and purpose.'

Respect those in charge

Many of the people we meet at church will be more experienced Christians than we are ourselves. We must recognise this and respect them. This particularly applies to the people who lead at church. It may be a mystery to you why these people are responsible for all that goes on, but there are probably some very good reasons why they are in leadership. We need to trust that God has put them in these positions for his purposes.

Respecting church leaders is a bit like respecting parents – it can be frustrating at times. Your parents might continually criticise your appearance, your choice of career, your friends or partner, how you raise your children or how often you phone them. You may feel they expect too much of you in other ways too – perhaps financially or practically. Hopefully, the ministers, pastors, priests or elders in your church will be more accepting and tolerant.

Perhaps the best way of honouring church leaders is to accept them, listen to what they have to say and accept their God-given authority. In other words, respect them because of their position, not their personality. Honour them by appreciating them in whatever way you can. If you have doubts or disagreements, or ideas to contribute, do voice them – respectfully, of course!

Be generous

In the New Testament times, churches were so full of generous people that the poor in the local community were fed and cared for. Just as God has given us much in Jesus, so we should be fantastically generous givers. In Luke 6:38 Jesus says: 'Give, and you will receive. Your gift will return to you in full – pressed down, shaken together to make room for more, running over, and poured into your lap. The amount you give will determine the amount you get back.' Let's be a church that is generous not only with our money, but with our time, skills and possessions.

Get involved

At its best, church is a vibrant, creative place where we learn how to live in community as God's family. It is a place where we worship, pray, engage with the Bible and serve – celebrating each other's differences and making some healthy, encouraging friendships. Church is a crucial base for recharging our spiritual batteries. It is through church that our lives will be infused with faith, hope and love. Church helps equip us to go back out into the world refreshed, to stand up for the poor, the oppressed and the downtrodden, loving them and sharing with them the Good News in both word and deed, as Jesus commanded.

Prayer

'Dear God, help me today to let go of any negative past experiences of church. Give me the courage to get involved and be real with the people I find there. I want to be teachable, encouraging and loving. Show me how to worship you in the life of your church. Amen.'

Further Reading

The Living Church, John Stott, Inter-Varsity Press, 2007
Holding Nothing Back, Tim Hughes, Kingsway Publications, 2007
Intelligent Church, Steve Chalke, Zondervan Publishing House, 2006
The Air I Breathe: Worship as a Way of Life, Louie Giglio, Multnomah, 2006

6

Power

The Power of the Spirit is Immense

When I asked Jesus into my life on 9 February 1975, I felt like I had woken up. Both my mind and heart were illuminated. Jesus had come into my life by his Holy Spirit, and it was as if all my arteries, which had previously been clogged up with hurts, habits and hang-ups, were cleared out and filled up with the presence and breath of Jesus. It is the power of the Holy Spirit that enables us to live out our soul purpose on this earth. In 2 Peter 1:3 we read: 'By his divine power, God has given us everything we need for living a godly life.'

A Little History

When Jesus promised his followers that he would send the Holy Spirit, he was promising someone who would stand alongside after the ascension (the time when Jesus went back up to heaven). This is borne out by what Jesus says the night before the crucifixion. In John 15 and 16, he uses the

Greek word 'paraclete' to describe the Holy Spirit. This word is difficult to translate into English but it basically means 'someone who stands alongside another'. Sometimes this word is translated as 'Counsellor', 'Helper', 'Comforter', 'Encourager' or 'Advocate'. In fact, the rest of the New Testament, and nearly 2,000 years of Christian experience, suggest that the Holy Spirit is all of these things.

Ten days after the ascension, at the Feast of Pentecost (when devout Jews offered to God the first produce of the year's harvest) the Spirit descended on the gathered disciples. And from then on everything changed. Counselled, helped, comforted and encouraged by the Spirit, the disciples started to spread the news of the risen Jesus. The message of Jesus was so powerful – and the disciples so enthusiastic – that the message spread fast and remarkably far, even though travel was slow and dangerous in those days. Within twenty years, churches were being founded throughout the whole of the Roman Empire and beyond.

If Jesus Christ was like a light to the world, the coming of the Holy Spirit was like pouring petrol on the flame. This is no exaggeration – the growth of the church in the first century, when so much was working against the early Christians, was absolutely extraordinary. It is no coincidence that

> *If Jesus Christ was like a light to the world, the coming of the Holy Spirit was like pouring petrol on the flame.*

this occurred immediately after Jesus sent the Holy Spirit upon his followers.

The Holy Spirit Today

The Holy Spirit continues to work among us today. In 1 Corinthians 6:19 Paul tells the members of the church in Corinth that the Spirit dwells in their bodies: 'Don't you realise that your body is the temple of the Holy Spirit, who lives in you and was given to you by God? You do not belong to yourself . . .' Just as the Spirit came to the first Christians at Pentecost, so the Spirit fills us when we make a commitment to Christ. His presence within us enables God's transforming work to take place within us. Other people notice him working in our lives. Why? Simply because the Spirit makes us Christ-like.

Who is the Holy Spirit?

You may have already begun to experience the work of the Holy Spirit for yourself. From the Bible, we learn the following about the Holy Spirit.

- The Holy Spirit is not merely a strange airy wind, spiritual force or influence. The Holy Spirit is God and has the characteristics of Jesus. After all, the Spirit could hardly be helping you in one place and me in another unless he was also God.
- At the same time, the Spirit is a person, which means that he is a 'he', not an 'it'. This is not simply a matter of grammar; we are able to have a relationship with the Spirit precisely because

he is part of the Trinitarian godhead (Father, Son and Holy Spirit).

- We will never be able to understand the Spirit entirely, because there are limits to our understanding of the spiritual realm. Instead, we need to deal with him humbly.

What Does He Do?

In terms of what the Holy Spirit does, we can say the following:

> *The Holy Spirit stands along-side Jesus' followers to help and support them.*

- The Holy Spirit stands along-side Jesus' followers to help and support them. Through him, we know Jesus' presence and power in our lives. 1 John 2:27 says: 'You have received the Holy Spirit, and he lives within you'.
- The Holy Spirit reveals the Father and the Son to us, and to those who do not yet know God. When we read the Bible, it is the Spirit who enables us to understand and receive its message.
- The Spirit speaks truth into our minds about God without drawing attention to himself, because his focus is always on the Father and the Son. He is 'transparent' in this respect. 1 John 2:27 continues: 'For the Spirit teaches you everything you need to know, and what he teaches is true – it is not a lie.'
- The Holy Spirit unites us with God and with other followers of Jesus. We can have fellowship

with God through the Spirit because the Spirit is actually God living in us. Romans 8:27 says: 'And the Father who knows all hearts knows what the Spirit is saying, for the Spirit pleads for us believers in harmony with God's own will.'

- Because the Holy Spirit is holy, he confronts sin. He brings light into the sin-obscured minds and hearts of those who do not know God, and reveals sin in the lives of Jesus' followers.

- In 2 Thessalonians 2:13, Paul describes the Spirit as: 'the Spirit who makes you holy'. Another way of describing this aspect of the work of the Spirit is to say that he sanctifies us.

- The Spirit brings us healing. As mentioned earlier, he is described in the Bible as one who counsels and comforts us. He makes us whole in body, mind and soul. 'For the Lord is the Spirit, and wherever the Spirit of the Lord is, there is freedom' (2 Corinthians 3:17).

- The Spirit equips and energises us for mission. It is he who gives us insight when we speak about Jesus. And only the Spirit can give us the ability to love those who are unlovable, while expecting nothing in return. 'For God has not given us a spirit of fear and timidity, but of power, love, and self-discipline' (2 Timothy 1:7).

- The Spirit acts as a guarantor of our future. His presence in us is evidence that as believers, we are indeed born again and belong to Jesus. Romans 8:2 says: 'And because you belong to him, the power of the life-giving Spirit has freed you from the power of sin that leads to death.'

Being aware of this, we are also reminded that just as Jesus rose from the dead, so we will also rise from the dead at the end of time.

- The work of the Spirit satisfies our souls. In John 4:14 we learn that Jesus said: 'those who drink the water I give will never be thirsty again. It becomes a fresh, bubbling spring within them, giving them eternal life.'

> *If you recently asked Jesus to come into your life, the important question now is what have you done with him?*

Why Have We Been Given the Holy Spirit?

If you recently asked Jesus to come into your life, the important question now is what have you done with him? Perhaps you don't want anyone to know that you are a Christian, and you have restricted the activity of the Spirit in your life. He is in your house, but you want to hide him in the basement. If so, it is fine for him to be there, but only so that he can help you clear out the cobwebs. When he has finished there, you had better take him up to the attic so he can clear out the junk up there, too. Then invite him into all the other rooms of your life!

The more you allow him to move in your life, the more you will experience his wonderful transforming power. Your heart will become full of 'love, joy, peace, patience, kindness, goodness, faithfulness, gentleness and self-control' (Galatians 5:22). These qualities are known as the 'fruit of the Holy Spirit'. Most people agree that these are universally tasty fruits.

Keep On Keeping On

Imagine that you are about to run a race. The starting gun sounds and you begin well, flying out of the blocks at a serious pace. But a short way along the track you seem to run out of energy. You try to keep going, but end up dropping out. If you have been running the spiritual race of Christianity for a while you may be finding that you are lagging in enthusiasm, the hurdles are too high to leap and the terrain is just too tough. God gives the gift of his Holy Spirit to everyone who wants to be in his team, enabling them to keep on going. The Holy Spirit will guide and help you in whatever you are facing.

A job advert in the newspaper said: 'Wanted – person to work on nuclear isotope molecular reactor counters, three-phase cyclotronic uranium photosynthesisers. No experience necessary.' Although that might sound challenging, know that if you have chosen to give your soul to God and live according to his purposes, the task he sets before us is even more demanding than this. But again, no experience is necessary. All we need is a willingness to hear and obey him, and to depend on the mighty power of the Spirit.

If the thought of living your life God's way looks impossible to you at the moment, be encouraged. The truth is that neither you nor I could ever do this in our own strength. But in 2 Corinthians 12:9 Paul reports the words of Jesus: 'My grace is all you need. My power works best in weakness.' The great apostle Paul was a man acutely aware of his own struggles and failings, and he saw that because of them, the power of God can work in him. He continues, saying: 'So now I am glad to boast about my weaknesses, so that the power of Christ can work through me. That's why I take pleasure in my weaknesses, and in the insults, hardships, persecutions, and troubles that I suffer for Christ. For when I am weak, then I am strong' (1 Corinthians 12:9,10).

Deep Healing Within

Have you ever had measles? If so, a rash appears all over your skin. Although this symptom is external, it is the result of a minuscule virus living inside your body. In order to be rid of the rash, you have to be rid of the virus. So it is with us as we struggle to live a life pleasing to God. We need to ask the Holy Spirit to bring us healing in the deep parts of ourselves where darkness and pain (sometimes the results of damage done to us by others in our past) reside. As this process starts to happen, we will begin to see change in our exterior behaviour.

I know many people with addictions: to smoking, shopping, pornography, sex, eating, not eating, drinking, masturbating and exercising, to name just a few. Few of us want to be addicted, but somehow we just can't shake the addiction off. In order to find freedom from our addictions and to take steps to change, we need to look to the root of why we do what we do. The gentle illuminating light of the Spirit helps us to see the roots of our actions. If we are willing for him to remove them, he will. Often this process takes months or even years.

On the other hand, sometimes the Spirit transforms us instantaneously. When a friend of mine became a Christian his language was immediately affected. Previously, his every sentence had been peppered with swear words. Suddenly, he found himself with no desire to swear. I am sure it took some effort on his behalf, too, but the Spirit enabled him to leave that part of his old self behind.

> *Suddenly, he found himself with no desire to swear.*

Revelation of Truth

Do you know any people who were born before 1940? It has been said that they were born before television, before penicillin, polio shots, frozen food, Xerox, plastic, contact lenses, videos, Frisbees and the pill. They were born before radar, credit cards, split atoms, laser beams and ball-point pens, dishwashers, tumble dryers, electric blankets, air conditioners, drip-dry clothes and before humankind walked on the moon.

Years ago, people got married first and then lived together. To them, fast food was something they ate at Lent. A big mac was an oversized raincoat and they had crumpet for tea. They lived much of their lives before many things came into existence – such as house husbands, computer dating, or dual careers. To them, a meaningful relationship meant getting along with the cousins, and sheltered accommodation was where they waited for a bus. They were born before day-care centres, group homes and disposable nappies. Their world was changed by

FM radio, tape decks, electric typewriters, artificial hearts, word processors, yoghurts and young men wearing earrings. For them, time-sharing meant togetherness, a chip was a piece of wood or a fried potato, hardware meant nuts and bolts and software was not a word. The term 'making out' referred to how you did in your exam. A stud was something that fastened a collar to a shirt and going all the way meant staying on a double-decker bus to the bus depot. Pizzas, McDonald's and instant coffee were unheard of. Thirty years ago, grass was mown, and coke was kept in the coal house. A joint was a piece of meat people ate on Sundays and pot was something they used for cooking. A gay person was the life and soul of a party and nothing more, while aids just meant beauty treatments or help from someone in trouble. It is no wonder some people sound old-fashioned when they speak!

Considering the distance that society has travelled since Jesus walked the earth, how is it that we continue to see God working in people's lives today? The explanation for this incredible reality is the work of the Holy Spirit. In John 14:17, Jesus says that the Spirit: 'leads into all truth'. Regardless of the culture or time in which Jesus' followers live, the timeless Spirit will reveal truth to them.

An Unchanging Spirit

Some things never change: children have snotty noses and their hands are sticky. Young people argue with their parents, fall in love and fall out with their friends, then back in with them again. People oversleep, worry too much and get obsessed with keeping up with the Joneses. In the same way, the Holy Spirit continues to be available for us, whatever the time, whatever the place.

> *Some things never change: children have snotty noses and their hands are sticky.*

Experiencing God

Are you still finding it difficult to believe that the Holy Spirit can really affect your life? Think with me for a moment about the ways in which we come to know and believe things in the world. There are three types of human knowledge: mathematical, scientific and personal. An example of mathematical knowledge is 5 + 5 = 10. Of course, there are plenty of other examples in the field of mathematics. This kind of knowledge is rational, logical knowledge. Then there is scientific knowledge. This is where you have a hypothesis and you carry out an experiment to see if your hypothesis is true or false.

There is one further type of knowledge to add to the above – personal knowledge. This is that which you know to be true yourself, because it stems from your own personal experience, but which you cannot explain or communicate to another person. All of these types of knowledge are valid. What a lot of people do today is take something that is personal and try and define it mathematically or scientifically. This is because there is the view that only mathematical or scientific knowledge is acceptable and 'true'.

But there is a problem with trying to explain everything in impersonal terms. Take kissing, for example. Would you agree that a kiss is personal? Can you define a kiss mathematically? No. Can you define a kiss scientifically? Yes, you can. It is the approach of two pairs of lips, with a reciprocal transmission of microbes and carbon dioxide. Now why don't you take someone out to dinner, then say: 'Let's draw our lips together and exchange microbes and carbon dioxide.' What do you reckon? Imagine you are in a very romantic restaurant and it is a very special moment. Your boyfriend or girlfriend might look at you and reply: 'Well, actually, I've got a cold at the moment so I could give you some special microbes.' You see, if you take something personal and you try and define it mathematically or scientifically you get a load of nonsense. God is personal. You don't prove God; you take a step of faith and experience him. And the Holy Spirit, too, is there for you to experience right now.

Evidence of the Spirit at Work

Are you seeing the fruits of the Spirit (the godly ways of thinking, speaking and acting that we mentioned earlier) being produced in your life? Fruit takes time to grow and often is hardly observed until ripe. As you start to look for evidence that the Spirit is working in your life, ask yourself regularly: 'How fruity am I?'

Recently, I have been enjoying walking in my garden, praying and thinking. Like the apple tree growing there, which produces apples because that is what apple trees do, so we will produce the fruit of the Spirit because that is the natural consequence of having the Holy Spirit living in us. We don't have to sit around, think about this fact or analyse it – it will just happen. So don't be despondent if you feel you haven't seen evidence of the Spirit in your life yet – be assured that with God rooted in your heart, fruit will eventually appear. We know this because in Matthew 12:33–35 Jesus said: 'A tree is identified by its fruit. If a tree is good, its fruit will be good. If a tree is bad, its fruit will be bad . . . For whatever is in your heart determines what you say. A good person produces good things from the treasury of a good heart, and an evil person produces evil things from the treasury of an evil heart.'

In John 15:5, Jesus says: 'I am the vine; you are the branches. Those who remain in me, and I in them, will produce much fruit. For apart from me you can do nothing.' We must be careful that our branch is never detached from the vine, or some disease will destroy our fruitfulness. We can sustain the work of the Holy Spirit in our lives by continuing to invest in our relationship with Jesus. When we do this, an abundance of fruit will be borne in our lives.

> *If a tree is good, its fruit will be good. If a tree is bad, its fruit will be bad.*

Achieving Amazing Things

The film *Chocolat* invites us into the community living in a sleepy little French village in 1959. In this village, everyone knows what is expected of them and if anyone happens to forget, someone provides a reminder. The villagers trust in the wisdom of ages past, including tradition, family and morality. The Mayor, Comte de Reynaud, is the self-appointed guardian of the town: he writes the preacher's sermons, guides the townspeople in their moral decisions and tries to maintain the status quo at all costs.

One day, a vibrant young woman arrives in the village. Her name is Vianne and she is anything but traditional. She does not go to church and she dares to open a chocolaterie in the middle of Lent. However, despite her lack of belief in God, her chocolaterie and her own gracious nature unexpectedly transform the town and its people. As the story unfolds, a wounded woman finds the courage to escape her abusive husband, a grandmother renews a broken relationship with her family members and even the Comte de Reynaud becomes 'strangely released' after an intense Easter Saturday chocolate conversion experience.

If a young woman selling chocolate could make that much of a difference to those around her – helping them to mend family relationships, break free from abusive situations and open their hearts to love – just think what a difference the Holy Spirit can make. If ever you doubt what he can achieve through you personally, remember the exchange between the angel and Mary in Luke 1:26–38:

> God sent the angel Gabriel to Nazareth, a village in Galilee, to a virgin named Mary. She was engaged to be married to a man named Joseph, a descendant of

King David. Gabriel appeared to her and said, 'Greetings, favoured woman! The Lord is with you!'

Confused and disturbed, Mary tried to think what the angel could mean. 'Don't be afraid, Mary,' the angel told her, 'for you have found favour with God! You will conceive and give birth to a son, and you will name him Jesus. He will be very great and will be called the Son of the Most High. The Lord God will give him the throne of his ancestor David. And he will reign over Israel forever; his Kingdom will never end!'

Mary asked the angel, 'But how can this happen? I am a virgin.'

The angel replied, 'The Holy Spirit will come upon you, and the power of the Most High will overshadow you. So the baby to be born will be holy, and he will be called the Son of God. What's more, your relative Elizabeth has become pregnant in her old age! People used to say she was barren, but she is now in her sixth month. For nothing is impossible with God.'

Mary responded, 'I am the Lord's servant. May everything you have said about me come true.' And then the angel left her.

God will do the impossible in us and through us if we allow faith to rise above human reasoning. We need to submit to God in the same way that Mary did. As we place our trust in God and his Word, he will work miracles and healing in our seemingly unchangeable situations . . . 'For nothing is impossible with God' (Luke 1:37).

> *God will do the impossible in us and through us if we allow faith to rise above human reasoning.*

Miracles Worked Through You

Miracles are rare, that is why we call them miracles. Yet are they rare because, like the spotted owl, they are an endangered species, or are they rare because it is difficult for God to find people who have faith and are willing to participate in a miracle? If receiving a miracle is dependent on our being submissive enough to put our lives in God's hands as Mary did, then perhaps we have our answer. When we keep things in our own hands, the outcome is predictable; but when we submit to God's ways, who knows what can happen! Yet, we need to do more than just put things into God's hands – we need to keep on offering him our very being.

'Bend Me O Lord!'

In 1904, a young student training for the ministry called Evan Roberts completely and totally surrendered his will to God's will, crying out to God, 'Bend me O Lord!' Evan returned to his home church to preach the message of revival, but his pastor was reluctant to allow him to speak. In a compromise, the pastor announced that Evan would be speaking following the regular prayer meeting and that anyone who wanted to stay would be welcome. Only 17 people stayed to hear Evan speak. Most of them were teenagers and young adults. Evan Roberts spoke in that church for nearly two hours with a four-point message that he was convinced could help bring God's revival:

1. Confess all known sin to God

2. Deal with and get rid of any 'doubtful' area of your life
3. Be ready to obey the Holy Spirit instantly
4. Confess Christ publicly

When Evan finished speaking, all 17 young people were on their knees crying out to God. They prayed until 2 a.m. that night and a move of God began. By the end of the week, over 60 people had turned to Christ and over the next 18 months revival swept through Wales. Over 100,000 people became Christians. The revival was so transforming that the national culture changed dramatically . . .

The taverns went out of business.

Work at the coal mines was brought to a standstill.

The mules that pulled the wagons were so accustomed to hearing foul language from the workers that after the men became Christians they didn't recognise their voices or commands.

The entire police force was dismissed for almost 18 months due to a complete lack of crime.

One of the few court cases that were actually brought before a judge was very unusual. The defendant came into the court and admitted his guilt, the judge led the man to Christ and the jury closed the case by singing a hymn.

The revival eventually made its way across the Atlantic and swept through parts of New York. There was even a daily column in *The New York Times* called 'Today's Converts', that listed those who had converted. What was it that made the Welsh revival so powerful and so fruitful for the kingdom of God? I think revival took place because Evan Roberts prayed for God to bend him. This prayer reflected a deep hunger for more of God and more of what only God can do. It was a submission to the complete purpose and plan of God, an open invitation to the Spirit to come and do whatever he willed. The power came because there was a reckless abandonment of self and an absolute embrace of all that God desired to do.

Our God is the same God who breathed life in Wales in 1904 and I believe he is still breathing life today. Not long ago I received a letter from a pastor letting me know about two people who came to faith and were healed at one of our meetings. Here is an extract from their testimony: 'Since that meeting our lives have completely changed. Even our families have noticed. It doesn't all make sense yet but it seems the Holy Spirit

> *Our God is the same God who breathed life in Wales in 1904 and I believe he is still breathing life today.*

is still doing something subtle in our lives. One of the amazing things is our healings . . . Gordon went back to the surgeon who said he no longer needed his foot amputated (because of an infected abscess) and I have started reading a book for the first time in 18 months.' Beryl, the woman who wrote this, was registered blind.

No Easy Solutions

Since the Holy Spirit shines a light into our lives, we must be prepared for what he will reveal. Although he has the power to cleanse us completely, his revelations may also be a bit of a shock to the system. Think back to Mary again. What do you think everyone else thought of her when she announced she was pregnant? She was supposed to be a virgin! An angel did appear to Joseph in a dream and explain the situation to him . . . but even with an angel to direct him, he had to make a courageous decision. He had to take for his wife a woman who was not bearing his child and, in so doing, share in the unjust shame that was heaped upon her. And he would also be undertaking to provide for the child and function in a fatherly role as he raised him. But Joseph did what the angel commanded him. Joseph's faith in God was what enabled him to overcome the stigma of becoming Mary's husband. He accepted both the stigma and the responsibility in order to do God's will – but it can't have been easy for him. In the previous chapter, we mentioned the fact that following Christ may well take us beyond our comfort zone. It is through the guidance and prompting of the Holy Spirit that we are led there.

Prompted by the Spirit

John Thomas Oaks was a musician in New York. On a chilly evening, he was playing at the Starbucks Café on 51st and Broadway. Friends had said to him that it was the most lucrative Starbucks in the world:

tips were good if you played well. John was playing tunes from the sixties on his keyboard, and singing with his partner. In particular he noticed one woman singing along. Afterwards, she asked if he knew any hymns. John picked 'His Eye is on the Sparrow'. Everyone in Starbucks listened attentively as they sang: 'I sing because I'm happy, I sing because I'm free. For his eye is on the sparrow and I know he watches me.' The people in Starbucks gave him thunderous applause. Then the woman turned to John and said, 'It is funny you picked that hymn. It was my daughter's favourite. She died last week of a brain tumour. She was 16. I'm going to be OK. I keep trusting the Lord and singing his songs.' Was all this just a coincidence of time, place, people and choice of hymn? Perhaps John was listening attentively to the prompting of the Spirit. Through the song that he chose he was used by the Spirit to bring comfort to a woman in desperate need.

Ask for More!

If you have already asked Jesus into your life then whether or not you feel you know it, the Holy Spirit is at work within you. However, Paul encourages us in Ephesians 5:18 to continually 'be filled with the Holy Spirit'. Just as a car needs to be refuelled with petrol in order to keep motoring along, so we need to ask for a fresh filling from the Spirit on a regular basis. Luke 11:10 says: 'For everyone who asks, receives. Everyone who seeks, finds.

> 'Be filled with the Holy Spirit.'

And to everyone who knocks, the door will be opened.' Pray to be filled with the power and the presence of the Holy Spirit every day. And when you sense his prompting, follow him in faith.

Prayer

'Holy Spirit, thank you for the incredible work that you do in so many lives. I ask you today to fill me with your love, goodness and power. Equip me to live my life God's way.

In particular, I now give you one specific area of my life that I am really struggling [or hurting] in. Would you start a process of healing and transformation in this. [Tell him now about one area of your life that you would like the Spirit to transform.] Renew me, restore me, and refresh me. Amen.'

Further Reading

Let The Healing Begin, Jeannie Morgan, Kingsway Publications, 2007
God Inside Out, Simon Ponsonby, Kingsway Publications, 2007
More, Simon Ponsonby, Kingsway Publications, 2005
Come, Holy Spirit, David Pytches, Hodder & Stoughton Religious, 1985
Changes that Heal: How to understand your past to ensure a better future, Dr Henry Cloud, Zondervan Publishing House, 1997
www.mindandsoul.info

7

Live it Out

What Does a Christian Lifestyle Look Like?

What springs to mind when you read the words 'Christian lifestyle'? Nuns or monks in strange, flowing garments? Geeky Christians with white socks and open-toed sandals? Pious friends who always seem to be at some church event or another and somehow manage to make you feel guilty about having a bit of a riot on a Saturday night? Before we go any further, can I say congratulations on making it into the first paragraph of this chapter – the thought of reading about what a Christian lifestyle looks like is enough to make most people run a mile!

Perhaps part of the reason that we have such a negative image of Christian living is the regular mockery made of Christians in our national press and media – the picture is always that a Christian lifestyle is simply about following boring, pointless rules (or doing so while behaving hypocritically). But turn your attention with me to a little verse in the Gospel of Luke . . .

One day an expert in religious law stood up to test Jesus by asking him this question: 'Teacher, what should I do to inherit eternal life?'

Jesus replied, 'What does the law of Moses say? How do you read it?'

The man answered, 'You must love the LORD your God with all your heart, all your soul, all your strength, and all your mind.' And, 'Love your neighbour as yourself.' 'Right!' Jesus told him. 'Do this and you will live!' (Luke 10:25–28)

Really Living

Jesus' words in verse 28: 'Do this and you will live!' excite me. Jesus is telling the expert in the law that if we live as he instructs, we will really 'live'. This is the recipe for life to the max! And take a look at a verse in Deuteronomy that follows shortly after the Ten Commandments: 'Stay on the path that the LORD your God has commanded you to follow. Then you will live long and prosperous lives in the land' (Deuteronomy 5:33). The message of the Old Testament reflects Jesus' words – if we live according to God's intentions for humanity we will live life to the full. These verses aren't saying that life as a Christian will be free from adversity, but that the best and most satisfying life that we could live is one lived according to the maker's instructions.

The only way to discover a truly satisfying life is to start living one out. So if you have recently begun a relationship with Jesus, the next step is to begin to put your faith in practice day to day.

> *The only way to discover a truly satisfying life is to start living one out.*

You Have Already Been Reborn!

Have you realised that because you have accepted Jesus into your life, a fundamental transformation has already taken place within you? Paul explains it like this: 'My old self has been crucified with Christ. It is no longer I who live, but Christ lives in me. So I live in this earthly body by trusting in the Son of God, who loved me and gave himself for me' (Galatians 2:20). Christ now lives in you – the 'old you' is dead! This transformation (or new birth) and the power of the Holy Spirit make possible the new lifestyle that you now want to start living.

We have already looked in previous chapters at the importance of starting to communicate with God in prayer, engage with him through the Bible and get involved with his people in church. But other aspects of your behaviour will need to change, too. Paul advised some young Christians: 'be careful how you live. Don't live like fools, but like those who are wise. Make the most of every opportunity in these evil days. Don't act thoughtlessly, but understand what the Lord wants you to do' (Ephesians 5:15–17).

Here is the essential about letting God change our behaviour: we need to invite him to change our thoughts first. In this chapter we will take a closer look firstly at what sort of thinking (or attitudes), and then behaviour (or actions), we need to develop as followers of Jesus.

Thinking Like a Disciple

A wife was asked: 'Do you usually wake up grouchy in the morning?' She replied, 'No, I usually let him sleep.' Sometimes in life, a sense of humour is essential – but cynicism is the most deadly disease on the face of the earth. Attitude is the mind's paintbrush – it can colour any situation. If we change our attitude towards life, our experience of living will change, too. Our circumstances might be the same, but if we have a Christ-like perspective, they may seem very different and we will start to be able to respond to them differently.

In the introduction to her well-known book *Battlefield of the Mind* (Hodder & Stoughton, 2007), Joyce Meyer writes:

Our actions are a direct result of our thoughts. If we have a negative mind, we will have a negative life. If, on the other hand, we renew our mind according to God's Word, we will, as Romans 12:2 promises, prove out in our experience 'the good and acceptable and perfect will of God' for our lives. The words on my computer mouse-mat remind me: 'Your attitude almost always determines your altitude in life.'

> *Our actions are a direct result of our thoughts.*

Paul expresses the importance of the way we think, which in turn affects our behaviour, in a prayer for the Christians living in Philippi:

I pray that your love will overflow more and more, and that you will keep on growing in knowledge and understanding. For I want you to understand what really matters, so that you may live pure and blameless lives until the day of Christ's return. May you always be filled with the fruit of your salvation – the righteous character

produced in your life by Jesus Christ – for this will bring much glory and praise to God.
(Philippians 1:9–11)

Paul is concerned about how the Christians in Philippi use their minds – he wants them to continue to develop in their knowledge and understanding of Jesus. And he wants them to 'understand what really matters': to think straight and get their priorities right. Paul sees that once these right attitudes are in place, these Christians will be overflowing with love, 'live pure and blameless lives' and be 'filled with the fruit of . . . salvation'.

As followers of Jesus, God makes a big ask of us. Our attitudes, he says, need to be the same as those of Jesus. 'You must have the same attitude that Christ Jesus had' (Philippians 2:5). In the next section of this chapter, we will take a look at the sorts of attitudes that Jesus displayed, and that the Bible encourages us to develop. Remember as you read that as we said in the previous chapter, the Holy Spirit is our engine for change. His incredible power can truly make the apparently impossible real in your life.

Humble Yourself Before God

It has been said that humility is 'not thinking less of yourself but thinking of yourself less'. Philippians 2:6–8 says of Jesus:

Though he was God,
    he did not think of equality with God as something to
    cling to. Instead, he gave up his divine privileges;

he took the humble position of a slave and was born as a human being.
When he appeared in human form,
he humbled himself in obedience to God and died a criminal's death on a cross.

Jesus – God who became man – was and is the true embodiment of humility. We need to make humility the starting point of our thinking, just as he did.

> *Jesus – God who became man – was and is the true embodiment of humility.*

The nineteenth century evangelist D.L. Moody wrote: 'I believe firmly that the moment our hearts are emptied of pride and selfishness and ambition and everything that is contrary to God's law, the Holy Spirit will fill every corner of our hearts. But if we are full of pride and conceit and ambition and the world, there is no room for the Spirit of God. We must be emptied before we can be filled.' Pride is so subtle that if we aren't careful we will be proud of our humility. We can easily become like the Sunday school teacher who, having told the story of the Pharisee and the publican, said, 'Children, let's bow our heads and thank God we are not like the Pharisee.'

Prioritise God

Being humble before God naturally means that we put him, his will and his way before our own. Do your priorities reflect your new commitment, your sole purpose in life? There was once a woman who totally and utterly failed to get her priorities right. She bought a parrot from a pet shop because she wanted a pet she could converse with. The next day she went back to the pet shop and said, 'The parrot is not speaking and you told me he would.' So the owner of the pet shop suggested she buy a mirror. She took his advice and took the mirror home. The next day she returned to the pet shop and said, 'The mirror didn't do it. He is still not talking.' The owner of the pet shop suggested she buy a ladder. 'He'll go up and down it,' the man explained, 'he'll look at himself in the mirror, go up, come down . . . that should get him talking.'

But the next day the lady went back to the pet shop again. This time the owner suggested she buy a swing which he was convinced the parrot would enjoy. The following day, she returned looking miserable. 'The parrot died,' she said. The owner of the pet shop was at a complete loss. Eventually, he asked, 'Well, did he say anything before he died?' 'He did actually,' the woman answered. 'He said: "Does that pet shop sell any food?"' The main thing in life is to remember the main thing.

Love God with Your Heart, Soul, Strength and Mind

In Luke 10:27, we read: 'You must love the Lord your God with all your heart, all your soul, all your strength, and all your mind.' This is Jesus' way of expressing the main thing. We must put God first in thought, word and deed, in business and in leisure, in friendships and at work, in the use of our money, time and talents.

Think about it like this: to be a Christian means you have got Jesus inside the car of your life. If you have already invited him in, the question now is this: where is he placed? Is he in the boot? If so, you drive your car to church, unlock the boot, get Jesus out for a religious happy hour, come out of the service and say, 'Get back in the boot!' Maybe you don't want anyone to know that you are religious, especially not your friends, colleagues or neighbours. Do you think of faith as a private thing, which doesn't need to be seen in your life?

Maybe you don't want anyone to know that you are religious, especially not your friends, colleagues or neighbours.

Is Jesus in the back seat, perhaps? If so, he is a bit more visible, but he is still only a passenger. Perhaps you like to direct most things in your life and just have the occasional friendly chat with the person sitting behind you as you drive along. You like to make your own decisions about where you are going in life, but you can see the importance of ongoing communication with Jesus. Does that sum up your relationship?

Perhaps Jesus is in the front seat. If so, he is even more visible, and can even seem a bit of a companion . . . but he is still a passenger. Someone who has this kind of relationship with Jesus might have a lot of communication with him and consider him a friend. But that person also reserves the right to make his or her own decisions.

In some people's lives, Jesus is in the driving seat. If that is you, you have taken him into your life and you are letting him direct the decisions you make. But watch out – are you a back seat driver? The car gets to a roundabout and Jesus turns right . . .

'Where are you going?' you ask.

'I'm going down Forgiveness Street.'

'I don't want to forgive her!' you say.

You get to a junction and Jesus turns left. 'Where are you going?' you ask.

'I'm going down the Road of Generosity.'

'I don't want to be generous,' you mutter.

Where is Jesus in the car of your life? If you think he is in the driving seat, make sure you constantly check he stays there, that he always has first place. To do that you will need to be aware of other people and priorities competing for his place each day.

To check that God really does take first place, ask yourself the following five questions. They come from the letters in the word 'first': F-I-R-S-T.

F is for Finances. Does God reign over your finances? The words in Deuteronomy 8:11–14, originally written to the ancient Israelites, apply equally to us: 'Beware that in your plenty you do not forget the LORD your God and disobey his commands, regulations, and decrees . . . For when you have become full and prosperous and have built fine homes to live in . . . be careful! Do not become proud at that time and forget the LORD your God.' Perhaps the reason why so many people have a love affair with money and possessions is because they do not have one with God. How we spend our money reveals what is important to us. All our money belongs to God and he wants us to give part of it back to him.

I is for Interests. Does God come first in terms of your interests? In life these may include your career, hobbies and recreation time. You can tell a lot about people's priorities by what they get excited over. What is it that gets you going? I find it interesting that if you jump up and down at a football match you get called a fan . . . but if you get the least bit excited in church, you are called a fanatic. (It is entirely illogical. Nevertheless, if you are called a fanatic for Jesus, you should take it as a compliment.)

What do you like to think about the most? What do you like to read about the most? What do you like to talk about the most? Our interests need to show our love for God because if it wasn't for God, we wouldn't be able to do anything. The apostle Peter writes:

> God has given each of you a gift from his great variety of spiritual gifts. Use them well to serve one another. Do you have the gift of speaking? Then speak as though God himself were speaking through you. Do you have the gift of helping others? Do it with all the strength and energy that God supplies. Then everything you do will bring glory to God through Jesus Christ.'
> (1 Peter 4:10,11)

R is for Relationships. Do you put God first in your relationships? In 1 Peter 1:13–15, we are told:

'think clearly and exercise self-control . . . live as God's obedient children. Don't slip back into your old ways of living to satisfy your own desires. You didn't know any better then. But now you must be holy in everything you do, just as God who chose you is holy.' If God is your number one, all your relationships will be affected.

S is for Schedule. Does God come first in your schedule? We can get so busy that we forget about God altogether, or put him at the bottom of the list. And don't just put him first on a Sunday. Imagine me saying to my wife: 'I've decided to be faithful to you on a Sunday, but I don't think I can do it for the rest of the week. Sorry.' Partial faithfulness is no faithfulness at all; God wants us to be faithful every day. Make regular appointments with him, as you would anyone else.

T is for Troubles. Do you go to God first when you are in trouble? We all go through problems and pressures, either minor ones or major ones. Minor troubles are the type you suffer from and major ones are what I have to deal with! (We all think our problems are bigger than other people's.) Putting God first in your life means asking him to help with the difficulties and hassles of life.

> *Do you go to God first when you are in trouble?*

Trust God

A hitchhiker with a really heavy rucksack was thumbing a lift. Someone stopped and said, 'Get in. Put your rucksack in the back.'

The hitchhiker says, 'No, it's OK,' and he tries to stuff the rucksack under the front seat, beneath his feet.

The driver says, 'What are you doing? Chuck it in the back.'

But the hitchhiker replies, 'No, it's really nice of you to give me a lift . . . but I'll carry my own rucksack.'

We are often similarly illogical when it comes to God. We say, 'OK, God. You take care of forgiveness and my destiny, and I'll take care of all my earthly troubles.' I'm not sure how you feel you are doing at putting God F-I-R-S-T, but chances are, you are finding it a terrifying challenge. Essential to our outlook as Christians is an attitude of trust. Our God is so much bigger and more powerful than you or me. We really can depend on him to watch over us, protect us and direct the course of our lives.

Are You a Worry-Head?

Many of us excel in worrying – me included! In his well-known Sermon on the Mount, Jesus taught his disciples to hand their worries over to him. 'Can all your worries add a single moment to your life? And why worry about your clothing? Look at the lilies of the field and how they grow . . . if God cares so wonderfully for wild flowers that are here today and thrown in the fire tomorrow, he will certainly care for you' (Matthew 6:27–30). Before you read any further, why not spend a moment handing over your worries to Jesus?

Humble Yourself Before Others

Luke 10:27 includes a second instruction: 'And, "Love your neighbour as yourself."' Choosing to love those around us as we love ourselves starts in our attitude towards others. Just as we humbly put ourselves second to God, we need to put ourselves second to other people. In Philippians 2:3 Paul says, 'Be humble, thinking of others as better than yourselves.' With this in mind, let's look at some other helpful attitudes towards others.

Don't just tolerate others, love them!

> *Tolerating others is currently an important message within our society.*

Tolerating others is currently an important message within our society. Jesus was certainly tolerant and we should follow his example in being non-judgemental, non-sexist, non-racist, non-ageist, non-classist and non-'type-of-person'-ist. Remember how Jesus behaved with the Samaritan woman he met at a well? Without batting an eyelid, he asked her if he could have a drink. In John 4:9 we read about her reaction: 'The woman was surprised, for Jews refuse to have anything to do with Samaritans. She said to Jesus, "You are a Jew, and I am a Samaritan woman. Why are you asking me for a drink?"'

Jesus went much further than simply tolerating people – he loved them unconditionally. Let's show our world that as followers of Jesus we love those who are different to us or even hate us. Luke 6:27

says: 'But to you who are willing to listen, I say, love your enemies! Do good to those who hate you.' Let's associate with all kinds of people – including government officials, poor people, the military, people with different religious beliefs, disfigured people, those suffering from disease and anyone considered an outcast by society. Let's show them that they truly matter, just as Jesus did.

Are you prejudiced?

In his autobiography, Mahatma Gandhi wrote that during his student days he read the Gospels thoughtfully and considered converting to Christianity. He believed that in the teachings of Jesus he could find the solution to the caste system that was dividing the people of India. So one Sunday he decided to attend a service at a church and talk to the minister about becoming a Christian. When he entered the church the usher refused to give him a seat and suggested that he go and worship with his own people. Gandhi left the church and never returned. 'If Christians have caste differences also,' he said, 'I might as well remain a Hindu.' That usher's prejudice not only betrayed Jesus but also turned a person away from trusting him as Saviour. If we don't accept and love those around us just as they are, how can we expect to help to introduce them to an all-loving God?

Do you struggle with being judgemental?

Let's not be too hasty about judging other people's behaviour. In Luke 21:1–4, we learn how Jesus felt about a woman who could give very little:

While Jesus was in the Temple, he watched the rich people dropping their gifts in the collection box. Then a poor widow came by and dropped in two small coins.

'I tell you the truth,' Jesus said, 'this poor widow has given more than all the rest of them. For they have given a tiny part of their surplus, but she, poor as she is, has given everything she has.'

There is a hill in the Lake District called 'Rash Judgement Point'. William Wordsworth named the hill. The story goes that while Wordsworth and his sister were standing at the top of the hill one day during the harvest season, looking down on the lake below, they saw a man in a boat fishing. Angered by this because the community needed every able-bodied man to be involved in gathering in the harvest, Wordsworth decided to go down the hill and challenge the fisherman for indulging in a leisure activity, when he should have been busy at work for the good of the local community.

Having called the man to the shore, Wordsworth noticed as he got out of the boat that he was old and bent over. Several fish lay in the boat. The man explained that, having worked for years gathering in the crops from the fields, he was now unable to do so because of his age and the pains that he suffered. Instead, in order to contribute to the life of the community at harvest time, he got up well before dawn and spent all day fishing the lake for fish to add to the community's resources. Wordsworth had passed judgement on the man without first giving him an opportunity to explain himself. Having listened to the man's explanation, he felt so convicted about the hasty judgement he had made that he named the hill from which he had first seen the man fishing 'Rash Judgement Point'.

Celebrate Your Differences

Remember to love the people who disagree with you on religious matters! John Wesley and George Whitefield were two great preachers of the eighteenth century evangelical revival, and were both great men of God. Sadly, having been great friends at Oxford, they

> *Remember to love the people who disagree with you on religious matters!*

fell out over the Armenian/Calvinist debate. (In summary, the Calvinists say that God chooses us, and the Armenians say that we are saved because we choose God – the truth is probably somewhere in the middle.) There was quite a bit of animosity between their followers. Once one of Whitefield's followers said to him: 'We won't see John Wesley in heaven, will we?' Whitefield humbly replied, 'Yes, you are right, we won't see him in heaven. He will be so close to the throne of God and we will be so far away, that we won't be able to see him.' What a lovely attitude Whitefield had. His humility was real. Despite profoundly disagreeing with Wesley, Whitefield recognised John Wesley as being a man of God. Indeed the respect for the other was so great that when Whitefield died, Wesley preached at his memorial service in London.

Be Forgiving

Sometimes you know that someone has done something very wrong; you may even have been personally affected by it. In the Bible there are 17 different instances of Jesus forgiving others – we need to follow his example. God came into the world not to rub it in but to rub it out. Therefore, we must not rub it in for others.

What about when somebody actually does something awful against us? Still we must find it in our hearts to forgive, just as The Lord's Prayer suggests we should do: 'Forgive us our debts, as we also have forgiven our debtors' (Matthew 6:12, NIV). How can we pray these words if we haven't already forgiven people who need our forgiveness?

> *What about when somebody actually does something awful against us?*

If you look at the word 'forgive' in the dictionary, you will see that three actions are involved in forgiveness:

- pardoning or releasing a person from punishment for a fault or offence;
- giving up any anger, resentment or vengeful feelings;
- showing mercy and compassion.

Forgiveness allows us to build something positive in the present. But it does not mean that we allow the same thing to be repeated in the future, or even that we ignore our own pain. We should work through the hurt caused, choosing to engage in the ongoing process of loving ourselves and the people involved in causing our pain.

Who Do You Need to Forgive Today?

If you are young – or even if you are old – it may be constructive to begin by forgiving your parents. They almost certainly did some things that hurt or upset you. Perhaps there is also some unresolved resentment between you, and maybe this is justified. You have a choice: either you forgive your parents and will then be free to live without resentment . . . or you live your life resentful. It is deeply painful to be betrayed or belittled by your own parents, but bearing a life-long grudge will not make anything better.

Forgive your parents, receive forgiveness from God and forgive yourself for any part you played in the difficult situation. If you sense there is still something wrong in your relationship with them, do as much as possible yourself to remedy the situation and pray for God's support while you do so. If your parents have already died you can still forgive and receive God's forgiveness yourself.

What if it is a Big Thing We Have to Forgive?

In 1993, 26-year-old Amy Biehl went to South Africa to help register black voters for their first free election. However, even though she was seeking to help the people of South Africa, as she was driving one day, she was dragged out of her car, stabbed and beaten to death by a mob committed to violence in order to overthrow the apartheid government. Soon afterwards, Amy's parents, Linda and Peter Biehl, gave up their jobs and moved from their California home to South Africa – not to seek revenge, but to start a foundation in Amy's name. Today, two of Amy's killers work for the foundation. They call Mrs. Biehl 'Makhulu', which means 'grandmother', because of the way she treats them. She says: 'Forgiving is looking at ourselves and saying, "I don't want to go through life feeling hateful and revengeful because that is not going to do me any good." We took Amy's lead. We did what we felt Amy would want.'

Bring About Reconciliation

Reconciliation not only forgives, it reaches out to restore. It pays back good for evil. It is following the heart and character of God, for we read in 2 Corinthians 5:18,19: 'God has given us this task of reconciling people to him. For God was in Christ, reconciling the world to himself, no longer counting people's sins against them.'

As we ask God to help us to reconcile others, so we will find ourselves wanting to make restitution to those we have hurt. Is there something from your pre-Christian life that you now realise you need to do something about? Have you ever filled in an insurance claim form and claimed for more than was necessary, called in sick when you weren't or borrowed things and not returned them?

Making amends is not easy, but we still need to do it. After all, the person who makes a mistake and doesn't correct it is making another mistake. We haven't been put on this earth to see through one another, but to see one another through. So let's do what we can to live at peace with everyone and let's do everything we can so that others can find peace with Christ.

> *Making amends is not easy, but we still need to do it.*

Be Supportive

There are times when people find it difficult to live well, even though they want to. They may be addicted or so rooted in their bad habits that they simply can't see a way out of their current situation. At times like that, we need to be supportive.

An exasperated father said to his son: 'When Winston Churchill was your age he worked hard at school all day and he studied his books at night.' And the teenage son replied: 'Yes, and when he was your age he was the prime minister!'

None of us are perfect but God still loves us. He expects us to do the same for our own imperfect family, friends and colleagues.

Once we were having Sunday lunch and the doorbell rang. I looked out of the window and said: 'Oh no. That's that man who talks out of his backside.' My wife let him in and one of my young sons said: 'You are that man that talks out of your backside.'

You know those moments when you just want to disappear? I had to say to my son: 'Daddy was wrong. You got the timing wrong, but I shouldn't have said that about that man.' It taught me a big lesson about making the effort to consistently support others.

Supporting other people may also involve giving them time. How often do you sit with people and really give them your attention? It may also involve giving them praise and encouragement, even if you wish that you too could experience their success.

Rejoice in the Successes of Others

I have heard it said that 'envy provides the mud that failure throws at success'. The story of Aristides the Just illustrates just that. Aristides was a soldier who was nicknamed 'The Just' because he was widely recognised as never seeking personal glory or financial gain in his public service to the people of Athens. One day, he was present at the Athenian assembly when that body voted that he should be banished. An illiterate man who was also there, not knowing who Aristides was, went up and asked him to write the name Aristides on his shell for him, meaning that he was planning to vote for his exile. As Aristides obliged him, he asked the man if he knew Aristides, or had anything against him. 'No,' the man said, 'I don't know anything about him, but I get tired of hearing him spoken of as Aristides the Just.'

Another ancient Greek legend tells of an athlete who ran well, but came second place in a race. The winner was embraced with praise and eventually a statue was erected in his honour. However, envy ate away at the man who came second. He resented the winner and he could think of little else, so he decided to destroy the statue of the winner. Night after night he went to the statue and chiselled away at the base, so as to weaken the foundation. But one night as he chiselled away, the heavy marble statue crashed down on him. He died beneath the weight of the marble replica of the man he had grown to envy. His own envy had destroyed him.

Let's rejoice in the successes and prosperity of others and instead of resenting other people's blessings, let's help extend them.

Develop an Attitude of Gratitude

Red magazine ran a feature entitled: 'Can't stop moaning, love a grumble . . . is it time you had a whingetox?' We humans love to have a good old moan, don't we? I used to think people complained because they had a lot of problems; I have come to realise that some people have problems because they complain. In Philippians 2:14, we are advised: 'Do everything without complaining and arguing'. So, instead of moaning about the negatives, let's notice the positives and give thanks. In 1 Thessalonians 5:18, we read: 'Be thankful in all circumstances, for this is God's will for you who belong to Christ Jesus.'

> *Be thankful in all circumstances, for this is God's will for you who belong to Christ Jesus.*

In Nehemiah 8:10, we read: 'for the joy of the LORD is your strength!' When we choose to remain in an attitude of joy, we find that life becomes much more enjoyable, whatever our circumstances. Studies have revealed that (regardless of their faith background) people who are daily grateful for the good things in life, however small, are often the happiest and most successful. And as Christians we have the living, powerful, perfect creator to thank!

So every time we feel inclined to complain, let's actively look for things to be thankful for . . .

The taxes we pay remind us that we are employed, the clothes that are a little too tight remind us we have enough to eat, the lawn that needs mowing, the windows that need cleaning and the gutters that need repairing remind us we have a home. The parking space we find at the far end of the car park reminds us we are capable of walking . . .

Our astronomical heating bills remind us that our homes are warm, the person behind us in church who sings off key reminds us we can hear, the piles of laundry and ironing remind us our loved ones are nearby. The alarm that goes off in the early morning reminds us we are alive, the exhaustion and aching muscles we feel at the end of the day remind us that we have been productive.

Feel Free to Be You

All this talk about praising God can seem very difficult to absorb – especially if you are facing tough or painful circumstances, or if you are depressed. While choosing to thank God for the good things in life can help us to begin to have a positive outlook, remember too that you are acceptable to God just as you are. We don't have to put on our metaphysical 'Sunday best' in order to come before God, or to gain the approval of other Christians. Jesus taught that being authentic is a good idea – he heavily criticised the Pharisees who, a bit like Hyacinth Bucket from the television series *Keeping up Appearances*, were not what they seemed. Our culture focuses heavily on the outside appearance of a man or woman – but Jesus tells us that what matters is the heart. Jesus offers liberation from the stress that comes from trying to be someone that deep down we know we are not.

Have You Ever Thought About What You Think About?

You can be sure that what you think about will be affected by who you usually spend time with (and what they think about), the books or magazines you read, the programmes and films you watch. If your thoughts are often on things that you suspect are not pleasing to God, developing an attitude of gratitude will be more of a challenge. At the end of his letter to the church in Philippi, Paul gives this advice: 'Fix your thoughts on what is true, and honourable, and right, and pure, and lovely, and admirable. Think about things that are excellent and worthy of praise. Keep putting into practice all you learned and received from me – everything you heard from me and saw me doing. Then the God of peace will be with you' (Philippians 4:8,9).

Perhaps you need to consider whether the things you fill your mind with are helping you to have godly attitudes? I'm not suggesting that you cut yourself off from culture and bin every film, CD or magazine that you own! But consider bringing this area of your life to God and ask him to guide you in what is right for you to absorb regularly. Don't be alarmed if at first you find it a real battle to say 'no' to old ways of thinking or behaving. Bring to God in prayer the areas that you are battling with and ask an older Christian for prayer. Be encouraged by verse 9 above: as we seek to fix our thoughts on good things, God brings us inner peace.

Don't Be Superstitious

Many people begin their day by looking at their horoscope. Will it be a day for love or staying away from difficult decisions? Did you know that superstitions can be a form of idolatry? Some people observe them from unconscious habit, and others believe that superstitions can actually protect them. Superstitions such as avoiding walking under a ladder, throwing salt over a shoulder or remarks such as 'touch wood' give respect to other powers at work. I noticed my hairdresser had a rabbit foot on a key ring. When I asked her about it she said: 'Oh, that is to bring me good luck.' 'But,' I responded, 'the rabbit wasn't lucky. Why on earth would you think that little rabbit's foot is going to bring you any luck at all?'

> *Did you know that superstitions can be a form of idolatry?*

Superstitions become dangerous when they rule people's lives. Some people get deeply distressed about a broken mirror or avoid making appointments on Friday 13th. Did you know that some hotels don't have a 13th floor because many people refuse to sleep there? (But we know that floor 14 is actually floor 13!) In Leviticus 19:26, we are told: 'Do not practice fortune-telling or witchcraft.' In verse 31 it also says, 'Do not defile yourselves by turning to mediums or to those who consult the spirits of the dead.' God knows that if we pursue these false paths, in the end we will find ourselves deceived and disappointed by what we experience. Are you following the god you want or the God who already is?

The Beatitudes

The Beatitudes are a set of teachings that Jesus gave during the Sermon on the Mount. They give a summary of the key attitudes and actions that we should look to develop as his followers. We have already unpacked some of these attitudes above – but many of them bring about actions, reminding us that we simply cannot separate our thinking from our behaviour.

> *We simply cannot separate our thinking from our behaviour.*

'God blesses those who are poor and realise their need for him, for the Kingdom of Heaven is theirs.
God blesses those who mourn, for they will be comforted.

God blesses those who are humble, for they will inherit the whole earth.

God blesses those who hunger and thirst for justice, for they will be satisfied.

God blesses those who are merciful, for they will be shown mercy.

God blesses those whose hearts are pure, for they will see God.

God blesses those who work for peace, for they will be called the children of God.

God blesses those who are persecuted for doing right, for the Kingdom of Heaven is theirs.

God blesses you when people mock you and persecute you and lie about you and say all sorts of evil things against you because you are my followers. Be happy about it! Be very glad! For a great reward awaits you in heaven. And remember, the ancient prophets were persecuted in the same way.'

(Matthew 5:3–12)

Most of these attitudes and actions go entirely against the grain of our world; at the moment they may well seem foreign to you, too.

Just Do It!

Some years ago, I had the privilege of meeting Mother Teresa and her Sisters of Charity in Calcutta. The month I spent with them had a deep impact both in my mind and heart. I heard many stories from the nuns, including many hugely amusing ones – they have a great sense of humour despite the pain and poverty they encounter in their ministry. I heard an interesting story about when Mother Teresa visited Australia. A novice to the monastery was assigned to be her guide and driver, and he was thrilled and excited at the prospect of being close to this godly woman. He dreamed of how much he would learn from her and what they would talk about.

However, during her visit he became frustrated because although he was constantly near her, she was always meeting other people. Finally, her tour was over and she was due to fly out to New Guinea. In desperation, the novice monk spoke to Mother Teresa: 'If I pay my own fare to New Guinea, can I sit next to you on the plane so I can talk to you and learn from you?' Mother Teresa looked at him.

'You have enough money to pay your air fare to New Guinea?' she asked.

'Oh, yes,' he replied eagerly.

'Then give that money to the poor,' she said. 'You will learn more from that, than anything I can tell you.'

The young man simply needed to learn by doing, because that – Mother Teresa knew – would transform his thinking, bringing about a deep change in his inner being.

Sometimes, we, too, simply need to get out there and get active for Jesus – boldly choosing to behave in new ways because of our new love for him. In Colossians 3:14, Paul says: 'Above all, clothe yourselves with love'. The imagery that he uses is of getting dressed. Don't worry if the clothing of Christ-like behaviour feels ill-fitting to you at the moment. Put it on courageously, and you will find that with time you will grow into it. In this final section of the chapter, we will look at some examples of what behaving in a Christ-like way in our society might look like.

Work Hard

Someone observed that the dictionary is the only place where you will find the word 'success' before the word 'work'. In Proverbs 21:5, we are also told that, 'Good planning and hard work lead to prosperity, but hasty shortcuts lead to poverty.' Pope John Paul II was asked: 'How many people work at the Vatican?' and he replied: 'About half.'

God intends for us to work. Note, though, that that doesn't necessarily mean having a job. Many people who work don't get a wage, but the work that mainly women and some men do in bringing up children is the most demanding and crucial of all. Volunteers also make an extremely valuable contribution. Today it is estimated that the UK volunteer population makes an annual contribution of £40 billion to the national GDP. And those who are disabled in some way need not fear because the emphasis in the Bible is not on criticising those who cannot work, but those who will not work due to laziness. So if you can work, WORK! Don't count the days, make the days count.

Be Honest

What's the difference between Jo Smith the convicted criminal and Jo Brown who lives down the road? A cynic would say the difference is that Jo Smith the criminal got caught, while Jo Brown didn't. God hates cheating and he delights in honesty.

> *God hates cheating and he delights in honesty.*

My friend Gary Grant, Director of The Entertainer (a chain of toy shops), got an unexpected delivery of toys worth £50,000. He hadn't ordered them, they just arrived. He rang his wife and said, 'What should I do?' She said, 'You know what you should do.' So he sent the whole consignment back. That is honesty (and integrity) for you.

Be a Good Employee

In Titus 2:9,10, the apostle Paul writes: 'Slaves must always obey their masters and do their best to please them. They must not talk back or steal, but must show themselves to be entirely trustworthy and good. Then they will make the teaching about God our Saviour attractive in every way.' Let's respect those in authority, refuse to take advantage of our bosses, work hard and resist the urge to nick stamps from the office supply!

Be Reliable

If you promise to do something, make sure you keep your word. In Psalm 37:21, it says: 'The wicked borrow and never repay, but the godly are generous givers.' Do you know the story of the two sons whose father wanted them to do some work (see Matthew 21:28–32)? The older boy initially refused, but then changed his mind and did the work anyway. The younger son immediately agreed to do the work, but ended up not doing it. Jesus makes it quite clear it was the son who actually did the work who had obeyed his father.

A Word on Sin

As we draw to a close in this chapter on the basics of living a Christian lifestyle, let's take a quick look at the thorny little issue of sin. In the book of Romans, Paul explains sin (our habitual destructive behaviours) in a comprehensive way. On the one hand, he says that as followers of Jesus we are cleansed of our sin and set free from the consequence of sin, which is death. The power of sin over us has been broken by Jesus' death on the cross. We see this in Romans 6:5–11:

> Since we have been united with him in his death, we will also be raised to life as he was. We know that our old sinful selves were crucified with Christ so that sin might lose its power in our lives. We are no longer slaves to sin. For when we died with Christ we were set free from the power of sin. And since we died with Christ, we know we will also live with him. We are sure of this because Christ was raised from the dead, and he will never die again. Death no longer has any power over him. When he died, he died once to break the power of sin. But now that he lives, he lives for the glory of God. So you also should consider yourselves to be dead to the power of sin and alive to God through Christ Jesus.

However, on the other hand, Paul says that because we are still human, we will always battle against sin. In Romans 7:15–17, he says:

> I don't really understand myself, for I want to do what is right, but I don't do it. Instead, I do what I hate. But if I know that what I am doing is wrong, this shows that I agree that the law is good. So I am not the one doing wrong; it is sin living in me that does it.

Be encouraged as you walk into the life that Jesus has called you to today. Although we will always struggle to live as Jesus did (simply because we are human), there is true victory in Christ.

> *Be encouraged as you walk into the life that Jesus has called you to today.*

Challenge Yourself

Which attitudes or actions do you need to change in order to think and behave like a disciple of Jesus? Imagine that Jesus, in physical person, was going to come and stay in your home. Would you be delighted to have him visit? Or would you be in a panic and have to meet him in the front garden for fear of what he would find in your home? Consider a few questions, presented in the form of a poem:

When Jesus came in would your welcome be sincere, or would you worry that this man had come too near?

Would you have to change your clothes before you let him in?

Would you hide some magazines and put a Bible where they had been?

Would you turn off the DVD and hope he hadn't seen the picture that was showing on your plasma TV screen?

Would you hide your world of music, tuck your CDs out of sight?

Would you rush about and tidy other things that were not right?

If Jesus chose to spend a day or two with you, would you choose to keep on doing all those things you often do?

Would you choose to keep on saying all those things you often say?

Would life for you continue as it does from day to day?

Would your family conversation lull, or keep its usual pace?

And would you find it hard each meal to say a table grace?

Would you sing the songs you always sing and read the books you read, and let him know the things on which your mind and spirit feed?

Would you take Jesus with you everywhere you plan to go, or would you maybe change your plans for just a day or so?

Would you be glad to have him meet your very closest friends or would you hope they had stayed away until his visit ends?

Would you be glad to have him stay forever on and on, or would you sigh with great relief when he at last was gone?

(Author unknown)

Feel Like You Don't Measure Up?

If you are anything like me, you know that there are many aspects to your thinking and behaviour that still need an overhaul from God! In fact, if you are thinking like this, it is a good thing. We will never fully get fixed, sorted and perfected until we reach heaven – we are works in progress for our entire lives.

If change feels like a real struggle, know that you are not alone. Sometimes we know that our old habits and attitudes are wrong, but we just don't want to live without them. Staying in a familiar, even if unpleasant, situation may be preferable to facing the pain or stress of healing and change – the idea of being set free by Jesus so as to change can seem terrifying. Remember that transformation is a process. We need to work on becoming a growing Christian over a period of days, weeks, months and years. Because we are dealing with change

> *Remember that transformation is a process.*

deep within, as well as in the face of the world's reaction to it, the process is not necessarily an easy one. God always stands with us through these challenging times.

Please also remember that in the meantime, God does not want us to wallow in guilt. So many young Christians today are burdened by an ongoing crippling sense of remorse for past mistakes. But the truth is that when we ask Jesus to forgive us, he forgives, and he forgets! Romans 8:1 says: 'So now there is no condemnation for those who belong to Christ Jesus.' Sometimes we struggle deeply to accept forgiveness from God. Do you need to do this today? If so, pray a prayer now telling God that you accept his forgiveness and you choose to forgive yourself, too.

There might be some parts of your heart that today are resisting change. Give God your tiny ounce of willingness and he'll do the rest – he truly can change your attitudes and actions. Depend on the mighty power of his Holy Spirit to help you, heal you and use you for God's glory.

Prayer

'Father God, I want to live a lifestyle that is pleasing to you. I trust that you can transform my attitudes and my actions. Please come by the power of your Spirit and give me the strength I need to live to delight you. Amen.'

Further Reading

The following books provide further wisdom on how to live a Christian lifestyle:

Live the Life, Mike Pilavachi with Craig Borlaise, Hodder & Stoughton Religious, 2006
The Call to Conversion: Why Faith is Always Personal but Never Private, Jim Wallis, Monarch Books, 2006
Velvet Elvis: Repainting the Christian Faith, Rob Bell, Zondervan Publishing House, 2006
The Smile of God, Andy Hawthorne, Kingsway, 2005
Uprising: A Revolution of the Soul, Erwin Raphael McManus, Thomas Nelson, 2006
The Purpose Driven Life, Rick Warren, Zondervan Publishing House, 2002
Walking with God: Searching for Meaning in an Age of Doubt, J.John and Chris Walley, Authentic Lifestyle, 2002
Ten: Living the Ten Commandments in the 21st Century, J.John, Kingsway Publications, 2000
Challenging Lifestyle, Nicky Gumbel, Kingsway Publications, 2001
Battlefield of the Mind, Joyce Meyer, Hodder & Stoughton, 2007
Also see Rob Bell's Nooma films: www.nooma.com

The following books are on specific lifestyle topics:

On forgiveness
Totally Forgiving Ourselves, R.T. Kendall, Hodder & Stoughton, 2007

Total Forgiveness, R.T. Kendall, Hodder & Stoughton Religious, 2001

For Christians at school
The Chocolate Teapot, David Lawrence, Scripture Union, 2004

On money
The Money Secret, Rob Parsons, Hodder & Stoughton, 2005

On work
God at Work: Living Every Day With Purpose, Ken Costa, Continuum, 2007

On sex and relationships
Sex God: Exploring the Endless Connections Between Sexuality and Spirituality, Rob Bell, Zondervan Publishing House, 2007
It's Always on my Mind, J.John, Authentic Media, 1998
Marriage Works, J.John, Authentic Media, 2008

The following books have been written specifically for women:

Created as a Woman, Beverley Shepherd, CWR, 2007
Finding Freedom: The joy of surrender, Helena Wilkinson, CWR, 2007
Worth Knowing, Survivor, Edited by Ali Herbert, Survivor, 2006

The following book has been written specifically for men:

Wild at Heart, John Eldridge, Thomas Nelson, 2001

8

Give it Away

Our Mission

When Queen Victoria was a child, she didn't know that she was in line for the throne of England. Her instructors, trying to prepare her for the future, were frustrated because they couldn't motivate her. Finally, her teachers decided to tell her that one day she would become the Queen of England. Upon hearing this, Victoria quietly said, 'Then I will be good.' The realisation that she had inherited this high calling gave her a sense of responsibility that profoundly affected her conduct from then on.

We Christians have a similar regal calling – we are 'Christ's ambassadors' (2 Corinthians 5:20). An ambassador is a representative who holds citizenship in one country and represents the interests of his or her country abroad. Sadly, some Christians have lost their sense of being ambassadors in this world and have become content to be ordinary citizens. But Jesus said to his followers: 'As the Father has sent me, so I am sending you.' Our citizenship is in heaven and we are to fulfil a mission here on earth as advocates and messengers of the King of kings, our Lord and Saviour Jesus Christ.

In a similar way to Queen Victoria, we are also heirs: we are due to receive a lavish heavenly inheritance from God our father. Romans 8:17a says: 'And since we are his children, we are his heirs. In fact, together with Christ we are heirs of God's glory.' How should we respond to this? Our response is to generously give back all that we have and are to God. Jesus lived a life of sacrifice on this earth, putting his own needs second to the needs of others, and giving up his own life so that we might live through him. We are called to be imitators of Jesus: to willingly give ourselves away as he did.

> *Our response is to generously give back all that we have and are to God.*

As we do this, we start to live out the purposes and plans that God has for our lives. In Ephesians 2:10, we read: 'For we are God's masterpiece. He has created us anew in Christ Jesus, so we can do the good things he planned for us long ago.'

It's Not Just About Your Cash

Did alarm bells ring in your head when you read the title of this chapter? 'Oh, no, a chapter asking me to give away all my money!' you might have been thinking. We looked briefly at the topic of being financially generous in Chapter 5, but in this chapter

I want to let you know that giving away what Jesus has given us is not solely about our finances. Jesus called us to join with him in building the kingdom of heaven, in helping others reconnect with God and experience the love of Jesus. In order to do so, we need to become profoundly generous in every way.

And how are we to do this? Jesus taught over and over again that the life mission of his followers should be to love others. He said: 'So now I am giving you a new commandment: Love each other. Just as I have loved you, you should love each other. Your love for one another will prove to the world that you are my disciples' (John 13:34,35). In Matthew 10:7,8, we read the words with which Jesus sent out his key followers, the twelve apostles. In them he expands on what their mission to love should look like in practice. He says: 'Go and announce to them that the Kingdom of Heaven is near. Heal the sick, raise the dead, cure those with leprosy, and cast out demons. Give as freely as you have received!' And before the resurrected Jesus left earth for heaven, he left these instructions with his followers: 'Go and make disciples of all the nations, baptising them in the name of the Father and the Son and the Holy Spirit. Teach these new disciples to obey all the commands I have given you' (Matthew 28:19,20).

These important teachings and Jesus' own behaviour demonstrate that our mission to love others means both caring for them in practical, sacrificial ways and also sharing his truth with them. We will explore these two elements of our mission as followers in more depth as this chapter continues. But first a word on servanthood . . .

Become a Servant

As we give all that we have and are to God through living out his love and grace, we become living sacrifices for him, and servants of Christ. In Romans 12:1, Paul writes: 'And so, dear brothers and sisters, I plead with you to give your bodies to God because of all he has done for you. Let them be a living and holy sacrifice – the kind he will find acceptable. This is truly the way to worship him.'

In May 1846, an evangelist called James Caughey visited a chapel in Nottingham, England and preached a sermon on the words Jesus is recorded as having said in Mark 11:24: 'I tell you, you can pray for anything, and if you believe that you've received it, it will be yours.' James Caughey preached that the key to this verse was to learn to desire God's desires, and that God's foremost desire was that we develop the character of a servant, help the poor and spread the gospel so that souls might be saved.

> *'I tell you, you can pray for anything, and if you believe that you've received it, it will be yours.'*

A young man was present at this service. He had started following Christ two years earlier, but had been drifting. However, that day in May God spoke to him through this evangelist, he felt a sense of compassion and also had a passionate desire to become God's servant. He then acted on God's directions and devoted himself to setting up an organisation committed to the salvation of souls and service to the needy. William Booth sensed that God had called him to become a servant of God, demonstrating his faith in both his words and actions.

It was this sermon on 'desiring servanthood' that inspired the young William Booth to fulfil his destiny and set up the Salvation Army. Years later, Booth wrote: 'I will tell you the secret . . . God has had all that there was of me. There have been men with greater brains than I, even with greater opportunities, but from the day I got the poor on my heart and caught a vision of what Jesus Christ could do with them, and me, on that day I made up my mind that God should have all of William Booth there was. And if there is anything of power in the Salvation Army, it is because God has had all the adoration of my heart, all the power of my will, and all the influence of my life.'

Mother Teresa is a woman whose life was a wonderful example of servanthood to Christ. She gave herself wholeheartedly to the poor, right up until her death. She said she simply believed that: 'We can do no great things; only small things with great love.' Such words are reminiscent of our Lord's words in Mark 10:43: 'Whoever wants to be a leader among you must be your servant.'

Sharing the Love of Jesus with Words

Following an exhilarating performance at New York's Carnegie Hall, celebrated classical cellist

Yo-Yo Ma called for a taxi to take him to a hotel and placed his cello – hand-crafted in Vienna in 1733 and valued at $2.5 million – in the boot of the taxi. When he reached his destination, he paid the driver, but forgot to take his cello. After the taxi had driven away, he realised what he had done. He began a desperate search for the missing instrument. Fortunately he had the receipt with the taxi ID number. After searching all night the taxi was located in a garage with the priceless cello still in the boot. Yo-Yo Ma's smile could not be contained as he spoke to reporters. Yo-Yo Ma, despite being exhausted, did not delay or postpone searching, but persisted because what was lost was too valuable to give up on.

The spiritually lost are too valuable for us to delay or postpone trying to reach them. Jesus pointed out that the thing that matters most to God is lost people. They matter so much to God that 'there is joy in the presence of God's angels when even one sinner repents' (Luke

> *The spiritually lost are too valuable for us to delay or postpone trying to reach them.*

15:10). There is more joy over one sinner coming to Jesus than over 99 people being right where they are supposed to be with God already. We are called to be generous with the truth. Are you willing to share the message of Jesus with others so that they too are given the opportunity to begin a relationship with him?

Research published by public theology think tank Theos just before Christmas 2007 showed that only 12 per cent of adults in Britain have a detailed knowledge of the Christmas story. A column entitled 'Xmas Really Is All About Spending' published around the same time in the *London Paper* debated the reason why we celebrate Christmas, and concluded: 'the meaning of this festival – is a triumphant display of material comfort for family and friends to fight the miserable cold. So the real point of Christmas is, after all, to spend money.' The fact that today's world has almost no clue as to the meaning of a festival that dominates almost a twelfth of our year is a sharp reminder that people in the UK do not know the message of Jesus and need to hear it as much as ever before.

Message Distribution

Coca-Cola is a product that has far outgrown its humble beginnings. In 1886, Dr John Pemberton first introduced Coca-Cola in Atlanta, Georgia in the US. The pharmacist concocted a caramel-coloured syrup in a brass kettle in his home. He 'distributed' it by carrying it in a jug down the street to the local pharmacy. Since 1886, surveys show that 97 per cent of the world has heard of Coca-Cola; 72 per cent of the world has seen a can of Coca-Cola; 51 per cent of the world has tasted a can of Coca-Cola. All due to the fact that the company made a commitment years ago that everyone on the planet should have a taste of their wonderful new drink. Is that not incredible? 97 per cent of the world has heard of this sugar and water concoction while

5 billion people in the world still need to be reached with the Good News of Jesus.

Some people are as passionate about sharing the gospel as the employees of the Coca-Cola company. Edith Burns, a Christian with a terminal illness, used to tell everyone she knew about Jesus. Her faith was so strong that when her doctor, a certain Dr Philips, called her in to give her some bad news about her condition, Edith said: 'Why are you so sad, doctor?' she asked. 'Are you reading your Bible? Are you praying?' Gently, Dr Philips said: 'Edith, I'm the doctor and you are the patient.' This made Edith burst out: 'Why shame on you, Dr Philips! Why are you so sad? Do you think God makes mistakes? You have just told me I'm going to see my precious Lord Jesus, my husband and my friends. You have just told me I'm going to celebrate Easter forever and here you are having difficulty giving me my ticket!' Dr Philips thought to himself: 'What a magnificent woman this Edith Burns is!' He knew that Edith had an interesting way of introducing herself to anybody new. 'Hello, my name is Edith Burns,' she would say. 'Do you believe in Easter?' Then she would explain the meaning of Easter. On many occasions people became Christians.

One day when Dr Philips walked into his office he had seen Edith talking to the nurse. In response to her usual question, Beverley had said, 'Why yes, I do.' 'Well, what do you believe about Easter?' Edith asked. 'Well, it is about chocolate eggs,' said Beverley. He had then heard Edith explain the real meaning of Easter. When she was admitted to hospital, Edith made a request. 'Doctor, I'm very near home, so would you please make sure they put women next to me who need to know about Easter?' He passed this on to the nurses, so Edith was able to continue to introduce many women to Jesus.

Everybody on that floor from staff to patients were so excited about Edith that they started calling her Edith Easter. That is, everyone except Phyllis, the senior nurse. Phyllis made it clear that she wanted nothing to do with Edith because she thought she was a religious nut. She had been a nurse in an army hospital and had seen and heard it all. She had also been married three times. She was hard, cold and did everything by the book.

> *She wanted nothing to do with Edith because she thought she was a religious nut.*

One morning, the two nurses who were to attend to Edith were sick. Phyllis had to go in and give Edith an injection. When she walked in Edith had a big smile on her face and she said: 'Phyllis! God loves you and I love you . . . and I've been praying for you.'

Not surprisingly, Phyllis said: 'Well, you can quit praying for me. It won't work. I'm not interested.'

'Well, I will pray,' said Edith. 'I've asked God not to let me go home until you come into the family.'

'Then you will never die because that will never happen,' snapped Phyllis, walking out of the room.

Every day Phyllis would walk into the room and Edith would say: 'God loves you, Phyllis, and I love you, too. I'm praying for you.' One day Phyllis said she was literally drawn to Edith's room like a magnet draws iron. She sat down on the bed and Edith said: 'I'm so glad you have come. God told me today is your special day.'

Phyllis said: 'Edith, you have asked everybody here the question "Do you believe in Easter?" but you have never asked me.'

'Phyllis,' said Edith, 'I wanted to many times, but God told me to wait until you asked. And now that you have asked . . .'

Edith took her Bible and shared with Phyllis the Easter story of the death, burial and resurrection of Jesus Christ. Then she asked: 'Phyllis, do you believe in Easter? Do you believe that Jesus Christ is alive and that he wants to live in your life?'

Phyllis replied: 'Oh, I want to believe that with all my heart. And I do want Jesus in my life.' Right there, Phyllis prayed and invited Jesus Christ into her life. Two days later, she went in to see Edith again. 'Do you know what day it is?' asked Edith.

'Why, Edith, it is Good Friday.'

'Oh no. For you every day is Easter. Happy Easter, Phyllis!'

Two days after that, on Easter Sunday, Phyllis came into work, did some of her duties and then went down to the flower shop to get some Easter lilies. She wanted to go and see Edith, give her some flowers and wish her a Happy Easter. When she walked into Edith's room, Edith was in bed. Her big Bible was on her lap. Her hands were resting in the pages of the Bible. There was a sweet smile on her face. When Phyllis went to pick up Edith's hand she realised Edith had died. Her left hand was on John 14:2,3: 'There is more than enough room in my Father's home. If it were not so, would I have told you that I am going to prepare a place for you? When everything is ready, I will come and get you, so that you will always be with me where I am.' Her right hand was on Revelation 21:4: 'He will wipe every tear from their eyes, and there will be no more death or sorrow or crying or pain. All these things are gone forever.'

Phyllis took one look at Edith's body and then lifted her face toward heaven. With tears streaming down her face, she said: 'Happy Easter, Edith. Happy Easter!' Phyllis left Edith's body, walked out of the room and over to a table where two student nurses were sitting. She said: 'My name is Phyllis. Do you believe in Easter?'

We Christians are an Easter people, living in a Good Friday world. We need to be as brave as Edith, approaching people in whatever way we can in order to help them meet Jesus. Are you willing to try communicating the Good News with those around you? You may hear some Christians saying, 'I'm not a natural evangelist, I'll leave that sort of thing to people like J.John.' But the truth is that if you are only willing, God will certainly use you. You don't need to be a public speaker. Be creative!

> *Are you willing to try communicating the Good News with those around you?*

In Colossians 4:5,6, Paul advises us: 'Live wisely among those who are not believers, and make the most of every opportunity. Let your conversation be gracious and attractive so that you will have the right response for everyone.' And when you approach anyone, don't be pessimistic about the influence you can have . . .

Small Actions Can Trigger Big Changes

In 1858, a Sunday school teacher called Mr Kimball led a Boston shoe clerk to give his life to Christ. The clerk was Dwight L. Moody who became an evangelist. In 1879, while preaching in England, a pastor called F.B. Meyer was transformed, who later went to an American college campus to preach. Through his preaching a student by the name of Wilbur Chapman became a Christian. Wilbur got involved in YMCA work and employed a former baseball player called Billy Sunday, to do evangelistic work. Billy Sunday preached in Charlotte, North Carolina.

Because the evangelistic meetings stirred the hearts of many people, around 30 businessmen wanted to devote a day of prayer for Charlotte. In May of 1934, a farmer let the men use his farm for their prayer meeting. One of the men, Vernon Patterson, prayed that 'Out of Charlotte the Lord would raise up someone to preach the gospel to the ends of the earth.' The businessmen then arranged for another evangelistic meeting inviting Mordecai Ham, a fiery evangelist who shattered the complacency of churchgoing Charlotte. The farmer who offered his farm as a venue for the prayer meeting was Franklin Graham, and his son Billy became a Christian during the Mordecai Ham meeting. In 1949 in Los Angeles, that boy, Billy Graham – who was now grown up – led a mission so fruitful it was extended. It was the mission which launched the world-wide ministry of Billy Graham. Is it not wonderful how our connections and seed-sowing can birth so much for the kingdom of God?

Lend Yourself to Jesus

As we think about the challenge of helping others meet with Jesus, let's hold in our minds what God has done for us. Dwelling on Christ's sacrifice for us reminds us that if we need to make a few sacrifices in order to share the Good News with others, it is worth it! An American friend, Dr Leighton Ford, said: 'Jesus was born in a borrowed manger, he preached from a borrowed boat, he entered Jerusalem on a borrowed donkey, he ate the last supper in a borrowed upper room and he was buried in a borrowed tomb. Now he asks to borrow the lives of Christians to reach the rest of the world. If we do not speak then he is dumb and silent. We need to lend ourselves to Jesus.'

It has been estimated that it takes 1,000 Christians 365 days to introduce just one person to Jesus Christ.

It has been estimated that it takes 1,000 Christians 365 days to introduce just one person to Jesus Christ. Can you imagine what would happen if 1,000 Christians spoke to one person about Jesus every year, let alone what would happen if we spoke to one person about Jesus just once every week? When we at Philo Trust researched 1,000 churches, we found that only 4 per cent of them had ever undertaken to do a course on evangelism. So what does that mean for us and our churches regarding global Christianity? There was a slogan I came across years ago: 'think globally and act locally'. I prefer to change it to: 'act locally and care globally'.

In particular, there is currently a need for people to share the Gospel in poorer countries. In under-developed countries, there is only one trained Christian worker for every 600,000 people, whereas in the West, the number is one for every 1,300 people. Did you know that 27 per cent of the world's population have not heard the message of Jesus, but only 2.5 per cent of the missions force is sent to these people? The nations that are home to the most people who have never heard the Gospel message are India, China, Pakistan, Indonesia, Iran, Thailand, Algeria, Morocco, Bangladesh and Nepal.

Sharing the Love of Jesus with Actions

Do your remember in Chapter 2 we thought about Jesus as our rescuer? If we can offer practical help and rescue for people in our world, we demonstrate the nature and truth of God to them. God not only brings us to himself, he also supports us and provides for us. In Isaiah 61:1 we read: 'The Spirit of the Sovereign Lord is upon me, for the Lord has anointed me to bring good news to the poor. He has sent me to comfort the broken-hearted and to proclaim that captives will be released and prisoners will be freed.' Here the prophet Isaiah expresses the mission that he felt called to by God – but these words are also a prophetic statement of the work that Christ would complete when he came to earth (Jesus applied them to himself in Luke 4:14–21). As people rescued by God, our mission is to rescue, heal and bring release to others.

1 John 3:16–19 says:

> We know what real love is because Jesus gave up his life for us. So we also ought to give up our lives for our brothers and sisters. If someone has enough money to live well and sees a brother or sister in need but shows no compassion – how can God's love be in that person?
>
> Dear children, let's not merely say that we love each other; let us show the truth by our actions. Our actions will show that we belong to the truth, so we will be confident when we stand before God.

For centuries, Christians have recognised the importance of this biblical message and have generously served the sick, poor and suffering in practical ways. In the Britain of the early nineteenth century, it was followers of Jesus such as William Wilberforce, Lord Shaftesbury and Hannah Moore who led the campaigns to abolish slavery and child prostitution, improve conditions in factories and prisons and found orphanages.

The Hands and Feet of Jesus

You may not have noticed them, but today, all across the world, there are Christians sharing the love of Jesus through their actions, while asking for nothing in return. In the USA, Charles Colson (a man who, before his conversion to Christ was considered by the media to be a politician 'incapable of humanitarian thought') has worked to reform the US prison service, and set up a movement of more than 50,000 voluntary prison workers operating in 88 countries. Six years ago in the UK, Maggie Ellis set up the first rape crisis centre in West Sussex. She explains her God-given conviction to do so, saying: 'It was a matter of justice. I couldn't live with the fact that in our county there really was no specialised service available, so I set something up.' Her centre now sees around eighty clients a week for counselling, all of whom have been sexually abused. The men and women who offer counselling and support to these people are motivated by their love for Jesus, and it is only through their dependence on him that they are able to cope with the harrowing stories of human destruction and oppression that they must hear. In Durban, South Africa, surfer Thomas Hewitt founded Umthombo, a charity working with street children in a city that has been called the 'new Rio'. Umthombo has seen the poverty-stricken lives of numerous children transformed – their team is now largely made up of former street children.

These are only a few stories of the millions of unsung heroes out there who are paying the price to spend their lives in sharing the message of Jesus through their actions. They follow the example of Jesus, who chose to take the difficult route of coming to earth and getting his hands dirty (and bloody) among fellow human beings. Are you prepared to get your hands dirty for him?

*They follow
the example
of Jesus,
who chose
to take the
difficult route
of coming
to earth and
getting his
hands dirty.*

Remember to pray to be guided by the Holy Spirit as you seek to help others, because only he can enable people to see that they are in desperate need of God's love and forgiveness. Only he can shed light into the darkness of people's minds. And as we serve, we must trust that our actions embody the love, truth and goodness of Christ and with time will have an impact. Often the old adage is so true: actions speak louder than words.

Stand with the Suffering

There was a fifth-grade class at a school in California that had 14 boys in it. The unusual thing about this class was this: all of them had no hair. Only one, however, had no choice in the matter. Ian O'Gorman was undergoing chemotherapy for lymphoma, and all his hair was falling out, so he had his head shaved. But then 13 of his classmates shaved their heads so Ian wouldn't feel out of place. Ten-year-old Kyle Hanslik started it all. He talked to some other boys, and before long they all went to the barber-shop. 'The last thing he would want is to not fit in,' said Kyle. 'We just wanted to make him feel better.' These boys were taking the advice in Galatians 6:2 (NIV), which says: 'Carry each other's burdens, and in this way you will fulfil the law of Christ.' Often, our simply standing alongside another in their time of pain or difficulty can have a profound impact.

What Would You Ask?

Imagine that someone walked up to you on the street and handed you a package with a million pounds in it. What would be the first thing you would ask the person who gave it to you? I know I would ask who the generous person was who gave me the money, and why on earth was I being given it? What you offer people in demonstrating and sharing Christ's love with them is worth infinitely more than a million pounds – and it is more than likely that as they realise the worth of the message of Christ, they will start to ask a few questions. But let's be people who are always willing to give away what is most costly to us, whether or not people ask us why we serve them. When they ask, let's be ready to tell them the reason for doing what we do.

Our call to love generously as Jesus did demands a revolution in both our words and our actions. Of course the two are intimately linked, after all, it was Jesus' words, the way he lived and the death he died that showed the world that he was the Son of God. So let's think outside the box about how to show Jesus to our world both visually and verbally. Sometimes we will need to demonstrate Jesus to someone with actions before we can speak to them about him. And sometimes it will be the other way around.

Called to Change the World

> *Our mission to love as Jesus did also extends into our role in the world in the wider sense.*

Our mission to love as Jesus did also extends into our role in the world in the wider sense. 'You are the salt of the earth,' Jesus said. 'But what good is salt if it has lost its flavour? Can you make it salty again? It will be thrown out and trampled underfoot as worthless' (Matthew 5:13). Jesus described his followers as salt because in his time there were no refrigerators, so the only way to preserve meat and keep it from rotting was to pack it in salt, which stopped decay. In other words, Jesus was saying that without God, our society rots. Morals become weak and living becomes self-centred.

We are called to bring the salty, society-preserving truth of Christ to our world as a whole – to get involved and make a difference. We need to stand up for truth and goodness and be prophetic, Christ-like voices in politics, in the media, in our workplaces and in culture at large. Martin Luther King Jr wrote in his book *Strength to Love* (Augsburg Fortress, 1963): 'The church must be reminded that it is not the master or the servant of the state, but rather the conscience of the state. It must be the guide and the critic of the state, and never its tool. If the church does not recapture its prophetic zeal, it will become an irrelevant social club without moral or spiritual authority.' If we want to be the salt of society, we must actively fight decay. We cannot remain passive and uninvolved.

So as a follower of Jesus, don't expect to be able to go quietly about your business without making an impact. In the passage after the one on salt, Jesus is recorded as having said:

> 'You are the light of the world – like a city on a hilltop that cannot be hidden. No one lights a lamp and then puts it under a basket. Instead, a lamp is placed on a stand, where it gives light to everyone in the house. In the same way, let your good deeds shine out for all to see, so that everyone will praise your heavenly Father.' (Matthew 5:14–16)

While salt has a negative role (in that it stops decay), light has a positive role: it illuminates and guides. Any Christian in any occupation can be salt and light – it is the Christian's job description – but it is not something you can do in part. Our call is to revolutionise our world for Christ and to inspire other people by living good lives. In James 3:13 we are told: 'If you are wise and understand God's ways, prove it by living an honourable life, doing good works with the humility that comes from wisdom.' If we compromise on this, our faith will lose its credibility. People will say: 'Why should I listen to you? Your life is just like mine!'

Remember, Jesus says you are the salt of the earth and the light of the world NOW – not you could be, or you will be once you get everything right in life. There is no reason to wait until later to speak up. What aspect of life in your community, circle of friends or group of colleagues could you get involved in and start to bring the love and values of Jesus to? Ask yourself now: are you salt? Are you light? The well-known ancient prayer of St Francis of Assisi draws a beautiful picture of what it looks like to be salt and light to the people around us. Why not read it now, praying it for yourself:

> Lord, make me an instrument of your peace,
> Where there is hatred, let me sow love,
> Where there is injury, pardon,
> Where there is doubt, faith,
> Where there is despair, hope,
> Where there is darkness, light,
> Where there is sadness, joy,
> O Divine Master, grant that I may not so much seek to
>   be consoled as to console;
> To be understood as to understand,
> To be loved as to love.
> For it is in giving that we receive,
> It is in pardoning that we are pardoned,
> And it is in dying that we are born to eternal life.

Beware a Few Pitfalls!

As you start to live out the mission Jesus gave his followers, you are likely to come across a few pitfalls that many of us have fallen into before! Here are a few words on how to avoid them.

1. Prepare yourself for opposition

However much you reflect the goodness of Jesus, there will always be people who oppose you. Martha Berry was a woman with a vision and a heart to help children. But she had no books, no building and no money. All she had was a dream to build a school for poor children. She went to Henry Ford to ask for a donation. Mr Ford reached into his pocket and gave Martha Berry just one dollar. Most people would have been insulted and perhaps given up then and

> *However much you reflect the goodness of Jesus, there will always be people who oppose you.*

there. But Martha took that one dollar, and bought a packet of seeds. She planted a garden, raised a crop, sold it and bought more seeds. After three harvests, she had enough money to purchase an old building for the children. She returned to Mr Ford and said, 'Look what your one dollar has done.' Henry Ford was so impressed that he donated a million dollars to Berry School. Prepare for some surprisingly heartless responses from others. Ask God to help you persist through tough times. We will look at facing adversity in more depth in the next chapter.

2. Don't lose sight of the Saviour

One leader said, 'It is sometimes easy to get busy and lose sight of the Lord of the work, while you are doing the work of the Lord.' Unfortunately, this has happened to too many people, and what they started out doing with passion ended up being shallow and insincere. Prioritise God before all else and strive to keep close to him. Forgetting why you serve or who you are serving is deeply demoralising.

3. Don't compromise

Sadly, we are sometimes slow to give the love and grace of Jesus away because of our tendency to compromise. In other words, we find an easy way out. Someone wrote: 'I was hungry and you formed a committee to investigate my hunger. I was homeless and you filed a report on my plight. I was sick and you held a seminar on the situation of the underprivileged. You have investigated all the aspects of my plight, yet I'm still hungry, homeless and sick.' Jesus has enormous compassion for the hungry, the homeless, the sick, the refugees, the casualties of injustice and the unemployed.

> *Jesus has enormous compassion for the hungry, the homeless, the sick, the refugees, the casualties of injustice and the unemployed.*

He wants to express this compassion through you and me, through his church. Let's not be people to push away the incredible privilege of the mission we have been given. Instead, let's pray that we will be able to use our personal advantages and abilities as opportunities to daily love others and contribute to the advancement of God's kingdom.

4. Create the time and space needed

How often have you heard people say: 'If only I had the time.' 'There is never enough time.' 'I don't know where the time goes.' 'I don't know where you find the time.' 'I'm hard-pressed for time.' 'I'll try to find time.' 'Is that the time already?' 'My, how time flies.' 'Could you fit in time?' 'I'm short of time.' 'Mustn't waste time, must we?'

Society tells us that the busier we are the more important we are. But if your body could talk, what would it say to you? Perhaps it is currently talking to you in the language of protest! And perhaps you are too busy to help others. How much time or space do you currently leave for spontaneous acts of love and generosity to those around you? I don't think any of us intentionally become too busy to help the lost. But Jesus said something interesting in the parable of the sower. Talking about seed being sown in Mark 4:18,19 (NIV), he said, 'Still others, like seed sown among thorns, hear the word; but the worries of this life, the deceitfulness of wealth and the desires for other things come in and choke the word, making it unfruitful.'

Other demands, responsibilities and possessions can choke out our fruitfulness and prevent us from helping other people to be fruitful, too. How can we prune the tree of our daily activities to leave time for rescuing the lost? How can we create gaps in our lives so that we can really see all the suffering going on around us, and actually do something about it?

A traffic warden came across an illegally parked car. He dutifully wrote out a ticket and completely ignored the man seated behind the wheel of the car when he placed the ticket on the window. The man in the car didn't react or make any excuses, he didn't argue and he certainly made no attempt to try and stop the traffic warden. There was a good reason for this: he was dead. He had been shot in the head 12 hours earlier, but was sitting up with blood on his face. The traffic warden was so preoccupied with ticket writing that he did not notice anything unusual. He just walked off to write another ticket. It is a shocking but true story. How different from that traffic warden are we?

Psychologists John Darley and Daniel Batson worked at the Princeton Theological Seminary in the US. Inspired by the story of the Good Samaritan (Luke 10:30–37), they decided to conduct a study. They asked groups of students to prepare a short talk on a given theme and to then walk individually to a nearby building to present it. The idea was that on the way to the presentation each student would see a man lying in an alley, moaning and groaning in pain. The researchers wanted to find out who would stop to help the man and also if being in a hurry would make any difference.

Half the students were asked to give a talk on ministry opportunities available for students after graduation. The other half was asked to prepare a devotional on the story of the Good Samaritan. One third of the group were told they would have plenty of time to get to the building to give their talk, a third were told they would just make it in time if they left straight away and a third were told they were already late – so they had better get moving immediately! In other words, the researchers put a third of their subjects in a 'low hurry' situation, a third in an 'intermediate hurry' situation and a third in a 'high hurry' situation.

The results were interesting. It made no significant difference whether the student was giving a talk on ministry opportunities or the Good Samaritan, but it did make a difference how much of a hurry he or she was in. Of the 'low hurry' subjects, 63 per cent offered help, compared to only 45 per cent of the 'intermediate hurry' subjects and 10 per cent of the 'high hurry' subjects. The researchers concluded that bystander apathy seems to be encouraged by the rush of life.

When I read through the Gospels, I am impressed by the relaxed pace Jesus kept from day to day. He moved through life so calmly and yet accomplished so much. Is there something we contemporary Christians have missed? Sadly, the result of our rushing is that we do not always use or even notice the opportunities entrusted to us. We pray for bigger opportunities while ignoring the people with needs right in front of us! When I am not rushing, I notice my neighbours and I chat to them. I talk to the people who serve me in the shop. I have time to go for a coffee with a friend who is feeling low. I have time to pray with someone at work who is unwell. Let's not be in too much of a hurry to help others. How could you slow down today and make yourself available to help someone else?

> *How could you slow down today and make yourself available to help someone else?*

5. Be in it for the long haul

Another good reason to make time to serve God is that sometimes reaping a harvest for God is a slow process; we need to be willing to stick around. As a child, Norman Geisler went to Sunday school because some neighbours invited him. He went back to the same church for Sunday school classes for 7 years – 364 Sundays in total. Each week he was faithfully picked up by a bus driver. Week after week he attended church, but never made a commitment to Christ. Finally, during his last year at school, after being picked up for church 364 times, he decided to commit his life to Christ. What if that bus driver had given up on Norman at 363? What if the bus driver had said, 'This kid is going nowhere spiritually, why waste any more time on him?' We often feel that the harvest seems far off, and we struggle to see even the flowers, let alone the fruit of our effort, but the harvest is promised. Don't give up! Continue to do what is right as long as you have the opportunity.

6. Respect your need for rest

Two woodsmen were on the way to work in the forest. As they walked, one woodsman challenged the other to an all-day tree-chopping contest. The challenger worked very hard, stopping only for a brief lunch break. The other man had a leisurely lunch and took several breaks during the day. At the end of the day, the challenger was surprised and annoyed to find that the other man had chopped substantially more wood than he had.

'I don't get it,' he said. 'Every time I checked, you were taking a rest, yet you chopped more wood than I did.'

'But you didn't notice,' said the winning woodsman, 'that I was sharpening my axe when I sat down to rest.'

Rest is not only vital to our spiritual lives, it is a necessity if we are to be effective. The fourth commandment says we must remember to observe the Sabbath day by keeping it holy. One day each week should be a day dedicated to the Lord. Even though Jesus was accused of breaking the Sabbath (because he healed people on it), he clearly understood this principle and made it a point to get away both with his disciples and by himself from time to time, in order to rest. In Mark 6:31, it is recorded that Jesus said to his disciples: 'Let's go off by ourselves to a quiet place and rest awhile.' He said this because there were so many people coming and going that Jesus and his apostles didn't even have time to eat. Resting was clearly Jesus' way of recharging his spiritual, physical and emotional batteries. But when you have had your rest, don't forget to get up and spring back into action!

> *Rest is not only vital to our spiritual lives, it is a necessity if we are to be effective.*

7. Remember we are grace-bearers

Sadly, over the years too many Christians seem to have left the crucial element of grace out of their behaviour. Writing to the early church at Ephesus, Paul wrote:

> Once you were dead because of your disobedience and your many sins. You used to live in sin, just like the rest of the world, obeying the devil – the commander of the powers in the unseen world. He is the spirit at work in the hearts of those who refuse to obey God. All of us used to live that way, following the passionate desires and inclinations of our sinful nature.
> (Ephesians 2:1–3)

Many people around us are 'dead' because of their disobedience to God, just as we ourselves once were. But we should focus on their need as a result of this state, not on their offences. After all, Paul continues: 'God is so rich in mercy, and he loved us so much, that even though we were dead because of our sins, he gave us life when he raised Christ from the dead. (It is only by God's grace that you have been saved!)' (Ephesians 2:4,5). The people around you who are miserable in their sin need a gentle, sensitive approach from you. Become part of their journey in discovering the Saviour Jesus for themselves by living out love and grace in every way.

Are You Giving Jesus Away?

John Wesley once said: 'Let us do all the good we can, by all the means we can, in all the ways we can, in all the places we can, at all the times we can, to all the people we can, as long as we can.' Think now about how you could give yourself away as Jesus did. Who could you share his message of love with? What small act of service could you do for someone today?

Prayer

'Lord, I want to embody your love, your goodness and your truth. Give me boldness to speak to others about your love, and courage to live out a grace-filled life. Show me how to make the time and space needed in my life to serve others as you did during your time on earth. Give me a heart like yours, overflowing with generosity. Amen.'

Further Reading

The following will inspire you in sharing the Good News of Jesus in words and actions:

Conspiracy of the Insignificant, Patrick Regan with Liza Hoeksma, Kingsway Publications, 2007
Worship, Evangelism, Justice, Mike Pilavachi with Liza Hoeksma, Kingsway Publications, 2006
The Irresistible Revolution, Shane Claiborne, Zondervan Publishing House, 2006
Out of the Salt Shaker and Into the World: Evangelism as a way of life, Rebecca Manley Pippert, Inter-Varsity Press, 1999
Actions Speak Louder: A Tearfund resource, with chapters by Mike Pilavachi, Tim Hughes and David Westlake. See www.tearfund.org/resources
Breaking News, J.John, Authentic Media, 2006
www.soulaction.org
www.justchurch.info

9

Adversity

The Problem of Suffering

A man was speaking in the open air in front of a crowd. 'People say there is a God, but I haven't seen him. People say Jesus is alive, but I've never seen him. People say that miracles happen, but I've never seen one.' Then another man spoke up: 'People say to me, the grass is green, but I haven't seen it. People say to me that the sky is blue, but I haven't seen it. People say to me that flowers are beautiful, but I haven't seen them. But you must appreciate . . . I'm blind.'

Many of us are spiritually blind. This may be because we put up barriers to seeing, or perhaps because we just don't want to see. There is one barrier to belief in God which confuses more people than any other and it is this: if God exists, why is there suffering in our world? If you recently became a Christian and told friends or family members about your new faith, you are likely to have already been asked this question. After all, Christians say that

God is all-knowing, all-loving, just and all-powerful. Reconciling a God like this with a world in which suffering exists is an even greater challenge.

Television cameras bring the suffering of the innocent into my living room daily. How come 40,000 children under the age of five died today because they didn't have enough food? Why are innocent people blown up by bombs, struck down by illness or crippled in accidents? Why didn't God do something when Hitler's henchmen drove 6 million Jews into the gas chambers? How come God allowed an avalanche of coal to engulf an entire school in Aberfan, Wales, killing 144 people, 116 of them children? (As a result of this event, *Punch* magazine ran a cover story entitled: 'Should God resign?') I have been a Christian for 33 years, but I can honestly say that I am still baffled by the mystery of a just and loving God who tolerates such injustice.

> *How come God allowed an avalanche of coal to engulf an entire school in Aberfan, Wales, killing 144 people, 116 of them children?*

Does God Intervene?

On the surface, God doesn't seem to be doing anything at all about suffering – so we are faced with a dilemma. Perhaps he is all-powerful and not all-loving: *if* he were loving, he would do something about suffering. Or, perhaps he is all-loving, but he doesn't have the power to intervene in earthly events.

Our culture adheres to two conflicting views on whether or not God does intervene in our world. On the one hand, many conclude that God doesn't act in our world at all. On the other hand, many blame God for anything that goes wrong in life. When something bad happens people say, 'Why did God let this happen?' But when something good happens, instead of giving God thanks, many people say, 'Aren't I lucky?'

Although it does not always appear to be the case, God does intervene in our world. The fact that he silently allows the human race to take the credit for our advances doesn't mean that he hasn't been ultimately responsible for them. A NASA director was explaining to a reporter how a module would land on Mars. The reporter asked the director how the module would return to earth. 'Ah, that involves a highly complex plan,' he explained. 'It begins with the words, "Our Father, who art in heaven".'

> *Is your assumption that God is distant from the world?*

Is your assumption that God is distant from the world – although, perhaps, you concede, he does occasionally intervene? Let's try turning that assumption on its head: perhaps the good God is constantly intervening in our world. If he stopped intervening, things would be significantly worse than they are now. Of course, this simplistic suggestion does not explain why God doesn't eradicate all suffering, but it might have jolted your thinking. In Romans 8:28, Paul gives us an insight into how he reconciles this problem in his own mind; he chooses to believe that God is in control: 'we know that God causes everything to work together for the good of those who love God and are called according to his purpose for them.'

But if God could intervene and put an end to all suffering, why does he allow it to exist?

The Bible makes it clear that suffering exists because of the sin of humankind; not because God is evil and likes to see humanity suffer. During an exchange some years ago in *The Times*, G.K. Chesterton (a correspondent) wrote concerning the nature of evil: 'Dear Sirs, You ask what is wrong with humanity. I am. Yours sincerely.'

The Fall

The origin of suffering goes back to the fall of Adam and Eve in the Garden of Eden. Because God is love, he made humans with free choice. Without freedom, the most meaningful and important things in life, such as friendship and love, would be impossible. When humans chose to turn their backs on God, they and the whole of creation became disconnected from the God of goodness and love. The door had been opened to sin and suffering entering our world – that is the tragedy of our independence.

Imagine a group of men in an aeroplane who are going to do parachute jumps. As they are putting on their parachutes, the supervisor says to one man: 'Now, you have got to make sure you attach this to your belt.'

The man says, 'I don't want to do that.'

The supervisor says, 'Look, if you don't do it, you are going to splat all over the pavement.'

So the man says, 'Well, I'll just jump out and test if that really does happen.'

We really can't ignore the maker's instructions without something going wrong. God could have made us without freedom of choice – he could have programmed us like a computer. That might mean a world without pain but equally it would mean a world without love. If you take away people's personal responsibility and freedom, you leave them less than human, like slaves, or puppets on strings.

What About Natural Disasters?

Our God-given ability to choose freely means that sometimes humans bring suffering upon one another, or themselves. But earthquakes, floods and other natural disasters can rarely be explained by a particular person's (or group's) destructive choices. The Bible indicates that the whole of creation has been affected by human choices made against God – redemption for our world in its entirety is needed.

What Can Be Done About Suffering?

You might well still argue that if God allowed free choice, and this in turn paved the way for suffering to enter our world, then God is ultimately responsible and he had better do something about it. Imagine that you were God. What would you do about the problem of suffering? Choose an action that is consistent with your character, but that does not violate the freedom of choice that you have given to men and women. May I suggest that there are two possibilities for you:

1. Wipe out this earth and start again. If you were going to hold on to your attributes and character as God on the one hand, and the freedom of choice of humanity on the other, really the only consistent thing would be to wipe out everything so that the problem no longer exists.
2. Decide to enter into your creation, now spoiled by humanity, in order to rescue people from it – that is what the New Testament is all about. The only way that this could happen is if God had a fifth attribute. The Good News is that he does. This attribute is described by the word 'grace'.

Grace

As we explored in Chapter 1, 'grace' means the undeserved favour of God expressed towards human beings. God expressed grace to humanity by entering into our situation. He intervened in our world in the ultimate way – by becoming a

> *God expressed grace to humanity by entering into our situation.*

man. God's answer and action in response to the problem of suffering came in the form of his son Jesus, and in his death on the cross.

Think again about the wooden cross and Jesus nailed to it. What do you see? You see the justice of God, because God must punish rebellion, greed and selfishness. If God didn't deal with sin, he would be sinful himself. Jesus was punished on the cross instead of you and me; so the cross is hard evidence for the love of God. In fact, the cross is the greatest expression of love that the world has ever known. 1 John 3:16 says: 'We know what real love is because Jesus gave up his life for us.'

The Eschatological Perspective

God created human beings for life without death, but because of the fall, death entered our world. When we choose Jesus and are forgiven, eternal life becomes ours once again, through Christ. God urges us in his Word to have an 'eschatological perspective' on life, which means to hold in our minds the end time when Jesus will return and restore the whole world to the perfect intentions of its creator. Our temporal 80 years of life on earth are simply a sneeze in God's eternal continuum. During the late nineteenth century in America, the black slaves, many of whom had a deep and profound faith in Christ, sang a song that begins with the well-known words: 'Swing low, sweet chariot, coming for to carry me home.' This was a plea to God to send his heavenly chariots down and sweep these suffering people up into the peace of heaven. They faced terrible, unjust suffering and yet because of their focus on their eternity with God, they were able to hold onto their faith and find joy in their circumstances.

We Won't Ever Fully Understand God

There are no glib answers to the problem of suffering. In the Bible, we read that God's wisdom and ways of working are infinitely greater than our own: '"My thoughts are nothing like your thoughts," says the LORD. "And my ways are far beyond anything you could imagine. For just as the heavens are higher than the earth, so my ways are higher than your ways and my thoughts higher than your thoughts"' (Isaiah 55:8,9). So it is no good shaking our fist at God expecting him to answer our questions before we will believe in him. Only if we go humbly to God can we begin to understand this question of suffering and know the reality of his presence in our own lives.

In the Bible, we read about a man called Job who experienced an enormous amount of unexplained suffering. God took him aside and said something like this . . .

'Job, I've got to talk to you. Were you there when I created the world? Your understanding of life is limited. You weren't there at the beginning. You do not see everything that is going on. You only see a tiny little bit of all that there is. Your understanding is incredibly limited. If you could see it from my perspective, you'd understand.'

And so it is with us. We need to accept that we have very limited vision.

Speak to any mature Christian and you will find that they still have unanswered questions and go through times of doubt about God, life and their faith. However, as Christians we have enough answers and enough truth to entrust our lives to a God who understands our struggles, questions and pain.

Why Do Christians Face Adversity?

> *But Jesus also taught his followers about the adversity – or difficulties – that they would face specifically because of their faith in him.*

We have considered the philosophical problems associated with the existence of suffering in our world. But Jesus also taught his followers about the adversity – or difficulties – that they would face specifically because of their faith in him. The story of Jesus calming the storm is a helpful visual metaphor for the challenges that lie ahead for all who have chosen to follow Christ:

One day Jesus said to his disciples, 'Let's cross to the other side of the lake.' So they got into a boat and started out. As they sailed across, Jesus settled down for a nap. But soon a fierce storm came down on the lake. The boat was filling with water, and they were in real danger.

The disciples went and woke him up, shouting, 'Master, Master, we're going to drown!'

When Jesus woke up, he rebuked the wind and the raging waves. Suddenly the storm stopped and all was calm. Then he asked them, 'Where is your faith?'

The disciples were terrified and amazed. 'Who is this man?' they asked each other. 'When he gives a command, even the wind and waves obey him!' (Luke 8:22–25)

Because these men followed Jesus and obeyed him, they found themselves in a tough situation – the storms of adversity literally came upon them. Just as they chose to ask for help in the face of the storm, so we too must turn to God during our stormy times. Jesus has power to overcome all things; we must choose to have faith whatever challenges we face.

The Cost of Discipleship

Jesus continually warned those he met that to follow him meant that they would suffer as he did. In Matthew 20:22, he asks them before his death, 'Are you able to drink from the bitter cup of suffering that I am about to drink?' He also said: 'It is easier for a camel to go through the eye of a needle than for a rich person to enter the Kingdom of God!' (Matthew 19:24). When Paul and Barnabas returned to Antioch (see Acts 14:21–23), they encouraged the new disciples there and reminded them of the same message: 'we must suffer many hardships to enter the Kingdom of God.'

In his inaugural address in Washington DC on 20 January 1961, John F. Kennedy said: 'Let every nation know, whether it wishes us well or ill, that we shall pay any price, bear any burden, meet any hardship, support any friend, oppose any foe to assure the survival and the success of liberty.' Are we, as Christians, willing to pay any price, bear any burden, meet any hardship, support any friend and oppose any foe to assure the coming of the kingdom of heaven?

Opposition and Persecution

> *Jesus' radical life of holiness and love brought about rejection and ridicule from others.*

Jesus' radical life of holiness and love brought about rejection and ridicule from others. If we choose a life like his, we too go against the tide of our world. We may even face persecution as we live lives that challenge the status quo and stand up for righteousness.

The Bible also warns us that we will face opposition from Satan as we seek to serve Christ. 'For we are not fighting against flesh-and-blood enemies, but against evil rulers and authorities of the unseen world, against mighty powers in this dark world, and against evil spirits in the heavenly places' (Ephesians 6:12).

Suffering in Response to Adversity

When we encounter adversity, we inevitably suffer. Just because we're Christians does not mean that we won't feel pain when we're hurt, or bleed when we're cut.

What Does God Think About Our Suffering?

God hates to see his people suffer. He chose and continues to choose to rescue people from suffering. We see this in the Old Testament story of God saving his people (the Hebrews) from their suffering under the corrupt Egyptian regime. God says, 'I have certainly seen the oppression of my people in Egypt. I have heard their cries of distress because of their harsh slave drivers. Yes, I am aware of their suffering. So I have come down to rescue them from the power of the Egyptians and lead them out of Egypt into their own fertile and spacious land. It is a land flowing with milk and honey' (Exodus 3:7,8).

Isaiah 49:13 also reminds us of the compassion and comfort that God brings to those who are suffering: 'Sing for joy, O heavens! Rejoice, O earth! Burst into song, O mountains! For the LORD has comforted his people and will have compassion on them in their suffering.'

However, just as Jesus allowed the disciples in the boat with him to face the storm for some time before he intervened, it seems that sometimes only suffering enables us to develop in the ways that we need to. At times, God appears to allow his people a level of suffering, perhaps as a reminder that we are to be dependant on him. A businessman once told me that he needed to have a car accident in order to wake up to the reality that he was ignoring his wife, his children and God. It is often suffering that draws out of people their true love and care for others.

A man found a cocoon and took it home because he wanted to watch the moth emerge from the tiny brown package. One day a small opening appeared. The man sat and watched the moth for several hours as it struggled to force its body through the little hole. And then it seemed to stop making any progress. It appeared that the moth had got as far as it could, and was stuck. So out of kindness the man decided to help: he took a pair of scissors and snipped off the remaining bit of the cocoon so the moth could get out. Soon the moth emerged, but it had a swollen body and small, shrivelled wings.

The man continued to watch the moth, expecting that in time the wings would enlarge and expand to be able to support the body, which would simultaneously contract to its proper size. Neither happened. In fact, that little moth spent the rest of its life crawling around with a swollen body and shrivelled wings. It was never able to fly. The man didn't understand that the restricting cocoon and the struggle required for the moth to get through the tiny opening were God's ways of forcing fluid from the body into the wings, so that the moth would be ready for flight once it emerged from the cocoon. Just as the moth could only achieve freedom and flight as a result of struggling, we sometimes need to struggle to become all that God intends us to be.

> *God doesn't always take away our problems and difficulties, but he does promise to be with us in the midst of them and to use them for good.*

God doesn't always take away our problems and difficulties, but he does promise to be with us in the midst of them and to use them for good. In 2 Corinthians 7:10 Paul says: 'the kind of sorrow God wants us to experience leads us away from sin and results in salvation.'

How Should We Face Adversity?

Actor William H. Macy in the film *Door to Door* portrayed the life of Bill Porter. Bill was born with cerebral palsy, which made it difficult for him to walk, speak clearly and to use his right arm. He was told that he would never be able to hold down a job or take care of himself. Social services labelled him 'unemployable'. They told him his only option would be to receive government disability support for the rest of his life.

Bill wouldn't listen and applied for a job selling household products door-to-door. At first, he was turned down, but he persisted. He offered to take the worst community in the city, just to have the opportunity to prove himself. Finally, he was given a job, but only on commission, no salary. Bill walked ten miles a day, ringing doorbell after doorbell, fighting against pain, weakness and fatigue – not to mention the difficulties of just communicating with people. When he made a sale, he had to have the customer fill out the order form, because he couldn't hold a pen to write. And yet, he succeeded. He became the company's top salesman, first in that city, then in the region and finally in the entire country. He achieved this even though he couldn't tie his own shoes or button his shirt. Imagine a man who has difficulty speaking and walking being able to make a career for himself as a door-to-door salesman for forty years! Bill displayed true heroism in the face of adversity.

All of us face situations where the deck seems to be stacked against us – situations where success, or even survival, seem questionable. But no matter how insurmountable the obstacles may appear, we have something far greater than Bill Porter's example on which to base our confidence. We have the promises of God to rely on; we have his presence and power at work in our lives. And that is more than enough to meet any challenge.

The prophet Jeremiah said:

> O Sovereign LORD! You made the heavens and earth by your strong hand and powerful arm. Nothing is too hard for you! You show unfailing love to thousands, but you also bring the consequences of one generation's sin upon the next. You are the great and powerful God, the LORD of Heaven's Armies. You have all wisdom and do great and mighty miracles. You see the conduct of all people, and you give them what they deserve.
> (Jeremiah 32:17–19)

> *Let's be people of faith who joyfully push on in the face of trials and hardship.*

Let's be people of faith who joyfully push on in the face of trials and hardship. As Paul says: 'I know how to live on almost nothing or with everything. I have learned the secret of living in every situation, whether it is with a full stomach or empty, with plenty or little. For I can do everything through Christ, who gives me strength' (Philippians 4:12,13).

Here are some practical and spiritual ideas for how to react when you face adversity or are suffering:

- Recall what Christ went through on the cross; this can bring great comfort. Hebrews 2:18 reminds us: 'Since he himself has gone through suffering and testing, he is able to help us when we are being tested.'
- Pray for God to intervene. We might also need to simply be quiet before the Lord, allowing him to speak into our hearts the words that will calm our fears. Did you know that God tells people in the Bible not to be afraid 366 times?
- If you are suffering physically (or someone you know is) you can ask for healing. God wants to bring healing and restoration to our minds as well as our bodies.
- Don't be surprised. 1 Peter 4:12,13 says: 'don't be surprised at the fiery trials you are going through, as if something strange were happening to you. Instead, be very glad – for these trials make you partners with Christ in his suffering, so that you will have the wonderful joy of seeing his glory when it is revealed to all the world.'
- Be courageous. It was not until I saw the movie *World Trade Center* that I realised how brave the rescuers were in the days following 9/11. Those rescue teams had to climb down into the chasms formed by broken concrete and steel to save trapped people. At any moment the massive wreckage above them could shift, trapping or killing them, too. And yet they did their duty. The American nation was right to honour them for their courage.

- Remember that God knows your limits. Paul wrote about his friend Epaphroditus with a feeling of desperation, 'Indeed he was ill, and almost died. But God had mercy on him, and not on him only but also on me, to spare me sorrow upon sorrow' (Philippians 2:27, NIV). God knows how much sorrow we can bear.

- Don't give up on what you are doing for God. Sometimes we are living well for God but when we face adversity we start to doubt our course of action. 1 Peter 4:19 says: 'So if you are suffering in a manner that pleases God, keep on doing what is right, and trust your lives to the God who created you, for he will never fail you.'

- Remember that God will protect you. David wrote: 'Who will protect me from the wicked? Who will stand up for me against evildoers? Unless the LORD had helped me, I would soon have settled in the silence of the grave. I cried out, "I am slipping!" but your unfailing love, O LORD, supported me. When doubts filled my mind, your comfort gave me renewed hope and cheer' (Psalm 94:16–19).

- Rejoice! The idea of rejoicing in the face of suffering seems like total madness. But as Christians, we are no longer dependent on things going well in our lives in order to be cheerful. Paul says: 'We can rejoice . . . when we run into problems and trials, for we know that they help us develop endurance. And endurance develops strength of character, and character strengthens our confident hope of salvation' (Romans 5:3,4).

- Hope, hope, hope! Romans 8:23 says: 'And we believers also groan, even though we have the

Holy Spirit within us as a foretaste of future glory, for we long to be released from sin and suffering. We, too, wait with eager hope for the day when God will give us our full rights as his adopted children, including the new bodies he has promised us.'

A Few Words of Advice for Specific Challenges

1. When you face spiritual attack

Many new Christians face intense spiritual opposition against their new faith. Suddenly it seems as if everyone and everything is conspiring against them putting their belief into action and telling others about it. If you feel like this, I encourage you to share what you are going through with an older Christian, and ask them to pray with you.

> *Many new Christians face intense spiritual opposition against their new faith.*

Also ensure that you put up some active resistance. Ephesians 6:10–18 (NIV) gives us a picture of how this works:

> Be strong in the Lord and in his mighty power. Put on the full armour of God so that you can take your stand against the devil's schemes . . . put on the full armour of God, so that when the day of evil comes, you may be able to stand your ground, and after you have done everything, to stand. Stand firm then, with the belt of truth buckled around your waist, with the breastplate

of righteousness in place, and with your feet fitted with the readiness that comes from the gospel of peace. In addition to all this, take up the shield of faith, with which you can extinguish all the flaming arrows of the evil one. Take the helmet of salvation and the sword of the Spirit, which is the word of God. And pray in the Spirit on all occasions with all kinds of prayers and requests. With this in mind, be alert and always keep on praying for all the saints.

People don't go to the bottom of the ocean without a diving suit. Similarly, Paul advises us not to go into the world without wearing God's armour. Try praying into this passage, asking God to protect you in the various ways described here.

2. When you are persecuted

In 2 Corinthians 6:8,9 Paul says: 'We serve God whether people honour us or despise us, whether they slander us or praise us. We are honest, but they call us impostors. We are ignored, even though we are well known.' How do we deal with situations when other people are clearly working against us? Forgiveness followed by fortitude is the answer. E.H. Chaplin wrote: 'Never does the human soul appear so strong and noble as when it forgoes revenge and dares to forgive an injury.'

Spend time dedicating your situation to God – Jesus taught us to pray for those who persecute us. If you are facing persecution, seeking prayer and support from other Christians

> *Spend time dedicating your situation to God.*

will be particularly important.

3. When you face difficulties in marriage

Forgiveness and fortitude are especially important in marriage. During the wedding ceremony many people say, 'I do' and then during their marriage they 'don't'. The Bible says: 'Didn't the Lord make you one with your wife? In body and spirit you are his. And what does he want? Godly children from your union. So guard your heart; remain loyal to the wife of your youth. "For I hate divorce!" says the Lord, the God of Israel' (Malachi 2:15,16).

There was a minister who was the principal of a college and his wife was struck down with Alzheimer's. Her health degenerated to the point where he could not take care of her, and run the college. And at the age of 59 he decided to give up his position as the principal of the college. His colleagues couldn't believe it. 'What are you doing?' they asked him. 'She doesn't even know who you are.'

He said, 'She might not know who I am, but I know who she is. She is the woman I made a promise to: until death do us part. I haven't got to care for her – I get to care for her.'

Trying times are not the times to stop trying. In a marriage it is important to treat all disasters as incidents, and none of the incidents as disasters. I am not suggesting our marriages will not have problems, but the kind of commitment that God is talking about means that when you hit a problem in your marriage, you face it and carry on together.

Leonardo da Vinci wrote: 'An arch consists of two weaknesses which, leaning against each other, make a strength.'

4. When you are wrestling with temptation

The first thing to understand about temptation is that it is normal. Satan's number one strategy is to intimidate us. It happens to everybody, but it is not a sin to be tempted. There are three common reactions when we're tempted:

1. Alarm: 'How could I think such a thing?'
2. Frustration: 'I keep failing in the same area.'
3. Discouragement: 'I'm never going to be able to change.'

Here are some suggestions for coping with temptation:

- Refuse to be intimidated. In Hebrews 4:15 we learn: 'This High Priest of ours understands our weaknesses, for he faced all of the same testings we do, yet he did not sin.' We shouldn't feel guilty for being tempted.
- Request help from God. In Psalm 50:15 we are told: 'call on me when you are in trouble, and I will rescue you, and you will give me glory'.
- Refocus your attention. Temptation begins with thoughts so we need to redirect our thinking. Sometimes we need to actively leave a situation – choosing to turn the TV or computer off. If we don't want to get stung, we need to walk away from the wasps.

- Confide in a friend. Ecclesiastes says two people are better than one, because if one falls down the other can help him up. But if someone is alone and falls, there is no one there to help him.
- Fill your mind with God's Word. The antidote to temptation is truth. It is interesting that when the devil tempted Jesus in the desert, Jesus said every time, 'It is written . . .' and then he quoted the Old Testament. We need to have a grasp of the Bible in order to be able to remind ourselves of the right course of action at any given point in life. When we have a grasp of the Bible, God has a grasp on us.
- Remember to live for the moment! Therese of Lisieux (1873–1897), a French nun, wisely said: 'I get in "soul trouble" when I focus too much on the past or the future. If I did not simply live from one moment to the next, it would be impossible for me to keep my patience. I can see only the present, I forget the past and I take good care not to think about the future. We get discouraged and feel despair because we brood about the past and the future. It is such folly to pass one's time fretting, instead of resting quietly on the heart of Jesus.'

Conviction Expressed Through Suffering

As we draw this chapter to a close, let's look back to Jesus' disciples. After Jesus had ascended into heaven, many of his followers suffered intense persecution for their faith and eventually died as martyrs. Yet don't think that these were people

> *Christians have been convinced enough about the existence of a true, loving and gracious God to die for their faith.*

with flawless faith or perfect lives – many times Jesus had helped them through their mistakes, mishaps and moments of unbelief. They were people just like you or me. From the first followers of Christ right up until today, Christians have been convinced enough about the existence of a true, loving and gracious God to die for their faith.

The Light in the Darkness

When it is dark you can see the stars. When you have nothing left but God, you begin to learn that God is enough. Look at Jesus during the dark times – because it is then that you will most clearly see his light. Romans 8:35–39 says:

> Can anything ever separate us from Christ's love? Does it mean he no longer loves us if we have trouble or calamity, or are persecuted, or hungry, or destitute, or in danger, or threatened with death? (As the Scriptures say, 'For your sake we are killed every day; we are being slaughtered like sheep.') No, despite all these things, overwhelming victory is ours through Christ, who loved us.
>
> And I am convinced that nothing can ever separate us from God's love. Neither death nor life, neither angels nor demons, neither our fears for today nor our worries about tomorrow – not even the powers of hell can separate us from God's love. No power in the sky above or in the earth below – indeed, nothing in all creation

will ever be able to separate us from the love of God that is revealed in Christ Jesus our Lord.

Our God promises to stand beside us in suffering. In his second letter, Timothy writes, 'But the Lord stood with me and gave me strength' (2 Timothy 4:17). I know that I would rather go through life with him there than without, even if I don't understand his every move. Let's actively choose to trust him, whatever life throws our way.

Prayer

'God, I praise you because you are sovereign and ruler of all. You have my life and this world in your hands. Bring an end to the suffering that so many people across the world are facing today. Please help me to lean on you in times of challenge, hardship and suffering. Amen.'

Further Reading

The Problem of Pain, C.S. Lewis, Fount, 2002
Where is God When it Hurts?, Philip Yancey, Zondervan Publishing House, 2002
Searching Issues, Nicky Gumbel, Kingsway Publications, 2001

10

The Road to Life

Journeying with God

A girl went off to university and didn't contact her parents for a long time. Eventually, she felt bad about this so she decided to write them a letter:

Dear Mum and Dad

Since I left for college I have been hopeless in writing and I'm sorry for my thoughtlessness in not having written before. I'll bring you up-to-date now but before you read on, please sit down. Are you sitting down? Don't read on unless you are.

I'm getting along pretty well now, despite the skull fracture and concussion that I got when I jumped out of my window when my dormitory caught on fire shortly after my arrival. My skull's pretty well healed and I only get the headaches once a day. Fortunately, an attendant at the petrol station witnessed the fire in my dorm and my jump to safety. He ran over, took me to hospital and continued to visit me there. When I got out of hospital I had nowhere to live because of the burnt-out condition of my room so he was kind enough to invite me to share his basement bedroom flat with him. It is sort of small and very cute. He is a fine boy and we have fallen deeply in love and are planning to get married. We haven't set the exact date yet, but it will be before my pregnancy begins to show.

Yes, Mum and Dad, I'm pregnant. I know how much you are looking forward to being grandparents and I know you will welcome the baby and give it the same tender care and devotion that you gave me when I was a child. The reason for the delay in our marriage is that my boyfriend has an infection, which I carelessly caught from him. I know, however, that you will welcome him into our family with open arms. He is kind and although not well-educated, he is ambitious. Although he is of a different race and religion than ours, I know that your often-expressed tolerance will not permit you to be bothered by that.

Now that I've brought you up-to-date, I want to tell you that there was no dormitory fire. I did not have concussion or a skull fracture. I was not in hospital. I am not pregnant. I do not have an infection and there is no boyfriend in my life. However, I have failed my exams and I wanted you to see these results in their proper perspective.

What the girl really wanted to say was: 'Dear Mum and Dad, I've failed my exams.' Sometimes it is difficult to make a fresh start in life, because other people's expectations weigh so heavily on us. This chapter is not only about making your fresh start happen (whatever the consequences)

> 'The gateway to life is very narrow and the road is difficult, and only a few ever find it.'

but also about how to see your new life with Jesus through to completion. Jesus said: 'the gateway to life is very narrow and the road is difficult, and only a few ever find it' (Matthew 7:14).

If you are young – or young at heart – the question of which road or direction to take in life is a hard one. It is an extension of that innocent-sounding question we ask children: 'What do you want to be when you grow up?' Over the years I have met many Christians grappling with questions like: 'How do I discover God's specific plan for my future?' 'What career am I called to?' 'How can I discern Jesus' voice and his way for me in this world?' And I hear Christians saying: 'I want to do great things for God, but I can't start because I don't know where I am going to end up.'

Your Life Plan

Has a friend ever asked you what your life plan is? I'm not talking about insurance here – but your dreams or ambitions for the future. Perhaps, before you became a Christian, you had life all mapped out: working your way up the career ladder, getting the great job, marrying the perfect man/woman, moving into your dream home, having the beautiful kids, buying the dog, the swanky car . . . and so on. As we have seen in previous chapters, when we meet Jesus, a shake-up of our values and plans begins to take place. For the first time, we ask God to show us his way for us, instead of marching blindly in our own self-selected direction. On the other hand, perhaps you are someone who has previously struggled to have the self-confidence to dream or see a future for yourself. Perhaps you find it quite overwhelming to hear that God wants to use you in incredible, beautiful ways, both to further his kingdom and to bring out the very best in you.

Wherever you are at in your thoughts on your future, there will be pressures shaping the course of your life in the present. Take a moment to reflect on what these might be, or who they are coming from. We all have people in our lives who consciously or subconsciously let us know just what direction they think our life should be going in. Or, we might be trying to keep up with all the latest fashions or hip lifestyle choices. We might be influenced by what celebrities are aspiring to. We might be trying to acquire the kind of social life that is apparently essential to a particular career choice. We might have adopted the attitude of friends that life is always about coming out on top, doing better, getting further, acquiring more.

In order to travel the road to life, you must neither live to please or impress others. Nor must you live to prove them wrong. We need to ask God to show us all the pressures and influences of the world that we have picked up on our journey so far – these are the things that will otherwise shape your future. If you haven't yet, I encourage you now to surrender all the plans

> *We need to ask God to show us all the pressures and influences of the world that we have picked up on our journey so far.*

and expectations you have for your future to God. Jesus said: 'If you cling to your life, you will lose it; but if you give up your life for me, you will find it' (Matthew 10:39).

God Has a Plan for Your Life

'"For I know the plans I have for you," declares the LORD, "plans to prosper you and not to harm you, plans to give you hope and a future. Then you will call upon me and come and pray to me, and I will listen to you. You will seek me and find me when you seek me with all your heart"' (Jeremiah 29:11– 13, NIV). God's plans and purposes for our lives are often so much higher than we realise. His plan for your life will make a positive difference in the lives of others.

Your Journey Along the Road to Life has Already Started!

I was on my mobile recently trying to sort out a problem with my bill. I was put on hold for what felt like hours, and meanwhile tinny music played out the same songs over and over in my ear . . . I expect you have experienced something similar! Sometimes, in seeking God's plan for our lives, we fall into the trap of thinking that until we have a clear instruction from God to do something very specific, we are on hold. But another look at what Jesus did here on earth reminds us that if we are to be like him, we have got plenty to be getting on with. Being a follower of Jesus is about journeying with him day-by-day, not living in limbo until he uses us in some great history-making moment. Try asking him every morning how you can live out his plan for your life that day. Don't wait for tomorrow to live out his plan for your life; start *now*!

> *Being a follower of Jesus is about journeying with him day-by-day.*

Back to Basics

I deliberately placed this chapter near the end of the book to help combat the sort of thinking described in the paragraph above. My hope is that through previous chapters, you will have begun to discover the new purpose and mission you have been given as a child of God, and as part of his family, the church. While it is important to seek God's specific direction for our individual lives, let's remember the essentials of Christian living. These things are like road signs and safety barriers alongside your road, and will help prevent you from wandering off it.

- We must hold on tightly to our guide to life. Although the Bible won't tell us what to do in every single situation we face, it does give us an enormous amount of clarity on the values to hold, what to prioritise and how to treat other people. You can be sure that integral to God's plan for your life is that you live according to his Word.
- Pray regularly! Ask God to guide you into the next small step that you are to take on your journey. Are you ready to do something that you

have never done before? Pray for a willing heart and for the courage, strength and determination to follow God today and in the future, whatever the cost.

• Continue to spend time with other Christians in the community of church – surround yourself with godly people who will advise you wisely.

Do You Ask God for Help?

A man came too close to the edge of a cliff, lost his footing and slipped over the side. As he fell, he desperately grabbed on to a bush. Filled with panic, he called out, 'Is there anyone up there?'

A calm, powerful voice came out of the sky, 'Yes, there is.'

The man pleaded, 'Can you help me?'

The calm voice replied, 'Yes, I can. What is your problem?'

'I fell over the cliff and am dangling and holding on to a branch that is about to break. Please help me.'

The voice from above said, 'Do you believe?'

'Yes, I believe,' said the man, still dangling.

'Do you have faith?' said the voice from above.

'Yes, I have faith.'

The calm voice said, 'Well, in that case, simply let go of the branch and I will catch you.'

There was a tense pause, and then the man yelled, 'Is there anyone else up there?'

Obviously, as well as asking God for help, we have got to be prepared to accept it when it is offered, however risky God's option looks. Isaiah 58:11 promises: 'The LORD will guide you continually, giving you water when you are dry and restoring your strength. You will be like a well-watered garden, like an ever-flowing spring.'

Adventuring with God

It is encouraging to remember that you are not the only person who's set out on the long journey with God into a better and different future. The Bible tells us about the journey that Mary, Joseph and Jesus took down to Egypt. It certainly wasn't a holiday – they weren't just 'going south for the winter'. Mary and Joseph were running away to save the life of their new-born baby because King Herod wanted him dead. The wise men who had visited the new-born Jesus had, unknowingly, tipped Herod off to the birth of a new king for Israel. Not understanding what kind of king Jesus really was, a jealous and probably insane King Herod wanted to eliminate what he thought was a threat to his throne.

When the wise men returned to their country by another route without reporting back to Herod, he was furious. In an act of horrible and senseless cruelty, he ordered all the boys up to 2 years old in Bethlehem to be put to death. So an angel of the Lord appeared to Joseph in a dream and told him to take Mary and Jesus away. He got his family up that very night, they quickly packed and left behind the comfort of familiar surroundings in Bethlehem to go to a distant and foreign land. This was not an

> *Mary and Joseph clearly had to trust that God would take care of them.*

easy journey to make – Mary and Joseph clearly had to trust that God would take care of them.

Given this kind of precedent, we shouldn't be surprised if on our journey with God, he sometimes takes us out of our 'comfort zone' – the place where everything is familiar and safe. God may well ask us to do things or go places that seem too challenging for us. God is the captain of our ship and he must steer the course of our lives. After all, as the old saying goes: 'A ship in harbour is safe . . . but that is not what ships are for.'

Some people think that being a Christian makes you dull, but in fact, life with Jesus makes you a serious, adventuring risk taker! The risks are calculated, however – we are on the same team as the God of the universe.

Think BIG!

Did you know that it is impossible to lick your elbow? Are you now trying to lick your elbow? I expect so – as soon as I read that, of course I tried it, too! If only we were as intrepid and as quick to try the apparently impossible when it came to living out God's purpose for our lives. The biggest Goliath in most of our lives is ourselves. (If you don't already know about Goliath – the warrior who a young boy called David fought and conquered – read 1 Samuel 17.) We wake up and look in the mirror every day and see the same person we saw yesterday, not the person God intended us to be, or is transforming us into. We don't look beyond the reflection and see the potential that God has placed in us. We are afraid and full of feelings of inadequacy.

Stretching our muscles often causes pain because it involves using old muscles more efficiently or using a new set of muscles altogether. If you are going to stretch yourself so as to go in God's direction, you may have to experience some personal discomfort and pain. Let God stretch you. If this talk of stretching makes you think of treks through the jungle or across the Himalayas, note that stretching yourself may look different for you than for someone else. You may need to show extreme patience or creativity. Your talents may not be what you imagine them to be, and even if you feel you have no talents at all, you may well be taken by surprise.

Your Contribution

One of the best ways to start discovering God's plans for you is to experiment with contributing your skills, gifts, talents or passions to God. If you are not sure what these are, a good way to find out is to start giving and see where it takes you. Let's take two real-life examples . . .

> *One of the best ways to start discovering God's plans for you is to experiment with contributing your skills, gifts, talents or passions to God.*

The first is the story of an unnamed Puerto Rican woman who felt she had nothing special to give. She joined an inner city mission in New York City, led by Bill Wilson, called Metro Ministries. (To give you an idea of just how violent a place this is, Bill Wilson himself has been stabbed and shot as he ministered to people.) This Puerto Rican woman told Bill: 'I want to do something to help with the church's ministry.' When he asked her what her talents were, she could think of nothing – in fact, she could hardly speak English. However, she said she did love children so Bill put her on one of the church's buses that went into communities and transported children to church.

Every week the Puerto Rican woman would find the worst-looking child on the bus and sit with them, whispering the words she had learned in English: 'I love you. Jesus loves you.' After several months, she became attached to one little boy in particular, but the boy didn't speak. Each week she would tell him all the way to Sunday school and all the way home, 'I love you and Jesus loves you.'

One day, to her amazement, the little boy turned around and stammered, 'I . . . I . . . I love you, too!' Then he put his arms around her and gave her a big hug. That was at 2.30 p.m. on a Sunday. At 6.30 p.m. on the same day he was found dead. His own mother had beaten him to death and thrown his body in a dustbin. 'I love you and Jesus loves you,' were some of the last words this little boy heard in his short life – from the lips of a woman who could barely speak English. This woman gave her one talent to God and because of that a little boy who never heard the word 'love' in his own home, experienced and responded to the love of Christ.

Rebecca Carranza is another woman who found something she could give to God. In 1950 she worked on the production line at the El Zarape Tortilla Factory in Los Angeles. Tortilla production had been automated and the machines could churn out twelve times more tortillas than anyone could by hand – but they also churned out many tortillas that were misshapen and apparently unusable. Rebecca saw something in the rejects that fascinated her so she began saving the discarded tortillas (which would otherwise have been thrown away). She used to cut them into triangles and fry them. Trying them out at a family party, they were an instant success. Rebecca Carranza went on to eventually run the El Zarape Tortilla Factory and she was the person who created 'tortilla chips', which have now become famous worldwide. She had the ability to 'see' something which everyone else considered worthless. She wasn't educated, rich or well connected, but she had vision – the kind of vision we all need so as to take what appears to be useless and transform it by the grace of God.

So if you are wondering what on earth your talents might be, aim to expand your horizons! And don't move into the future looking over your shoulder. Learn from your past, but be full of hope for what might be. If our God is a God of transformation, then there really is no reason why you should do things tomorrow in the way you did them yesterday.

Question Yourself

As you consider your future road with God, start imagining where you might go. Answer the following questions honestly, perhaps jotting down your answers in your journal.

- If you were to state your goals in life, what would you say?
- What opportunities are available to you at the moment?
- In an ideal world, where do you want to be this time next year?
- Are you going in the direction you want to? If not, what might be stopping you from taking a new course?

You might find these questions challenging to answer – especially if in the past you were not the sort of person to sit down and think clearly about your future. Asking an older Christian to listen to your answers to these questions and to pray with you about them might be helpful. Here are a couple more to get you thinking.

- Which habits do you want to develop and how would making these changes benefit you, other people or your relationship with God?
- If you were to describe the kind of friend / sister / brother / student / employee / housemate / mother / father (pick one or two that are relevant to you) that you want to be, what would you say?

- Which aspects of your character would you like to see change and who would this benefit?
- Who do you want to share the Good News of Jesus with this year?
- If you were to state one clear (and possibly small) step that you need to take along the road to life now, what would it be?

God-Given Vision

We can't change how we came into this world but we can change how we leave it. Helen Keller was once asked, 'What would be worse than being born blind?' to which she replied: 'Having sight without a vision.' What a profound statement by a woman who was born into this world deaf, dumb and blind. Helen could not change how she came into this world, but she could change how she left it.

Vision is the ability to see, and as Christians we gain vision by looking at God. The old saying is true: 'If you aim at nothing, you will hit it.' So visualise what you are aiming for and you are much more likely to hit your own personal target. Try writing your vision down by spending ten minutes drawing a wild spider diagram, noting down your passions, the options open to you now, your dreams and the things you would like to achieve one day. Pray before you start and then dedicate what you end up with on your piece of paper to God. Trust that

> *As Christians we gain vision by looking at God.*

he will continue to speak to you about what you have scribbled down.

When we understand how awesome God is, we will not hesitate to ask him for great things. Vision includes a faith to believe that 'I can do everything through [Christ], who gives me strength' (Philippians 4:13, NIV). Develop a vision that includes the faith to believe and the courage to act.

Keep Refocusing on God

> *While you are developing vision, it is vital to give control to God.*

While you are developing vision, it is vital to give control to God. This is a continuous, ongoing process that should endure throughout our Christian lives – seeking God for renewed vision and handing over control to him. In Isaiah 30:19–21 we read God's promise to re-envision us when we ask:

'O people of Zion, who live in Jerusalem, you will weep no more.

He will be gracious if you ask for help.

He will surely respond to the sound of your cries.

Though the Lord gave you adversity for food and suffering for drink, he will still be with you to teach you.

You will see your teacher with your own eyes.

Your own ears will hear him.

Right behind you a voice will say, "This is the way you should go," whether to the right or to the left.'

Have you ever wondered why a pigeon walks the way it does? According to an interesting article I once read, the reason is so that it can see where it is going. A pigeon can't adjust its focus as it moves, so it has to bring its head to a complete stop between steps in order to refocus.

As we walk with the Lord we have the same problem as the pigeon. We have a hard time seeing while we are moving. We need to stop between steps and refocus on where we are in relation to the world and the will of God. That is not to say we have to stop and pray and meditate about every little decision in life. But our walk with the Lord needs to have a built-in pattern of stops included in it, which enables us to see more clearly before moving on.

Do You Need to Wait?

Psalm 27:14 gives some wise advice: 'Wait patiently for the Lord. Be brave and courageous. Yes, wait patiently for the LORD.' Listening to God and waiting to know what is right is sometimes harder than taking action. Let's be people who can hold in tension the fact that sometimes we need to act, and at other times we must be willing to wait patiently on God.

There is Always an Element of Doubt . . .

Are you looking for 100 per cent certainty about God's leading, before you are willing to act? Remember that faith always makes space for some doubt – otherwise it wouldn't be faith! If you had concrete certainty about your future or your calling then you wouldn't need a God to guide you. Trusting God means both that we wait on him for guidance, direction and leadership – and then we get going in the direction he points us in, using our intelligence and our talents. Don't let a few doubts stop you; they simply show that you are human!

Don't Bin Your Common Sense!

When we are doing what we feel is God's will, we must not forget our normal knowledge of the world.

> *When we are doing what we feel is God's will, we must not forget our normal knowledge of the world.*

There is a Middle Eastern saying relevant to us as Christians: 'Trust in God, but tie your camel first.' Obviously, a camel is likely to wander off if it is not securely tethered, just as all kinds of other things are likely to go wrong if we don't use our usual common sense when dealing with matters of God and the world. We mustn't be stupid and naïve.

In Luke 16:8–9 we are told: 'it is true that the children of this world are more shrewd in dealing with the world around them than are the children of the light. Here's the lesson: use your worldly resources to benefit others and make friends. Then, when your earthly possessions are gone, they will welcome you to an eternal home.' God has generously given each one of us talents and we should use them. (Have you read the parable of the talents? If not, see Matthew 25:14–30.)

All Callings Have the Same Value to God

Often we hear wonderful stories of Christians who have felt called to travel to the other side of the world or do something with their life that is radically different from the norm. If God calls you in this way, you must be obedient. But don't forget that Jesus and his disciples were called to serve their neighbours and people in nearby towns and villages. Jesus simply saw the needs in those around him – for forgiveness, healing, love, relationship with God – and he met them. Part of Jesus' calling was to work as a carpenter, while Paul made tents when he wasn't preaching.

God has unique plans for everyone. Your vision might look quite different to your friend's, although neither should be at odds with the teaching and direction of the Bible. No one calling is higher or more holy than another – you can just as much be called by God to be kinder to your brother, as to train to be a policeman or to start helping out in your local homeless shelter.

A friend of mine is a journalist. She reminds herself regularly that she is a Christian first, and a journalist second. Inevitably, this affects both the minor decisions she takes in the workplace and the more major decisions affecting her future career. What matters is the way in which we conduct ourselves, whatever situation or job we are in. In Colossians 3:17 we read: 'whatever you do or say, do it as a representative of the Lord Jesus, giving thanks through him to God the Father.'

The Bright Lights of Success

Dig a little deeper into your motivations for the choices you make in life and you may well find that a fear of failure and a desire for success are key factors behind all that you do. If you are a new Christian, realigning your thinking about success will be an important adjustment to make. Success with God in the picture is no longer about ticking the world's boxes that measure achievement. It is not about making money, being popular or living the dream life. Success with God is living in obedience to him. Success is pleasing God with what we do. Success is being the best we can be while recognising that to be perfect would not allow space for God! To be successful you don't need to be a perfectionist – you simply need to be a depend-on-God-ist!

As we have seen in the chapter on adversity, becoming a Christian is no guarantee of an easy or apparently successful life (in the world's understanding of the word). However, you might well find that on becoming a Christian, you do start to be more successful in what you do. It is logical: you have a new motivation in life. You now want to live your life Christ's way. You have found your sole purpose and so living becomes something you will want to do with more gusto! You may well apply yourself better to your studies or job, respect your boss more than you did previously, and as a result see your grades improve or your pay packet increase. But instead of your successes bringing you pride and glory – as they might have done before you knew Jesus – allow them to bring glory to God.

Thank him for them and be humble about them. God is responsible for everything we have and are – don't forget that you couldn't achieve anything without him.

A Word on Failure

You might have heard Christians say: 'there is no such thing as failure with God, only the opportunity to learn'. And they are right! If you have been unable to step out and do the things that you feel called to do because of a fear that you will mess them up or fail, it is time to let go of that crippling belief! As you know, when we mess up we ask Jesus for forgiveness and he forgives and forgets. We cannot fail – we can only make a mistake, realise it, ask for forgiveness and help to change, move on and try doing it a new way! The Bible is full of stories of people who some might see as failures, but whose situations God redeemed – Moses, David, Gideon and Jonah, to name a few.

What Kind of Old Person Do You Want to Be?

Have you ever answered that question? Think for a minute about what sort of character you would like to have when you grow old and grey (or get a blue rinse). Sometimes in life we get really wound up about what to study, what career to pursue or what relationships

The Bible is full of stories of people who some might see as failures, but whose situations God redeemed.

we want in the here and now, when we could well do with spending some time thinking about how our character is developing. How important will your fear of failure or striving for success today be in twenty-five or fifty years' time? If you were to fast-forward through life to being very old right now, what would you think as you reflect back on where you are today?

Recognise God-Incidents

Does it ever occur to you that the coincidences in your life could be 'God-incidents'? God has been arranging encounters in human history since the beginning of time. For example, take the story of the doctor who was sitting at his desk one morning sorting through the mail and papers, which his housekeeper had laid out on his desk. Most of what he read he threw into the wastebasket. Then he noticed a magazine, which wasn't even addressed to him, but delivered to his office by mistake. It fell open to an article entitled 'The Needs of the Congo Mission'. Casually, he began to read and was suddenly consumed by these words: 'The need is great here. We have no one to work the northern province of Gabon in the central Congo. And it is my prayer as I write this article that God will lay his hand on one – one on whom, already, the Master's eyes have been cast – and that he or she shall be called to this place to help us.' Dr Albert Schweitzer closed the magazine and wrote in his diary: 'My search is over.' He gave himself to the Congo.

That little article, hidden in a periodical intended for someone else, was placed by accident in Dr Schweitzer's mailbox. By chance he noticed the title and it leapt out at him. Coincidence? I don't think so – it was a God-incident. If we are seeking God, he will intervene to keep us on the road that he has planned for our lives.

'Close the Doors, Lord'

As I approach making significant decisions in life, I often pray that God would open the metaphorical doors into the rooms that he wants me to enter, and close doors to me, too. The results can be dramatic. A friend of mine recently began to feel called by God to work for her church. At the time, she was doing well in her city job and there seemed no logic to leaving her workplace. She prayed that if this was the next step that she should take in life, that God would close the door on her current job. God answered her prayer swiftly: the next day she was made redundant with little apparent reason! She started work in the church soon afterwards.

Make Sure You are Fully Alive

It is impossible to be a half-hearted Christian. In Revelation 3:15 we read: 'I know all the things you do, that you are neither hot nor cold. I wish that you were one or the other!' We must wake up so that we are fully alive, asking

> It is impossible to be a half-hearted Christian.

God to help us to be zealous for him in every area of our lives. Jesus' words are recorded earlier in Revelation: 'I know all the things you do, and that you have a reputation for being alive – but you are dead. Wake up!' (Revelation 3:1,2).

The Russian novelist Fyodor Dostoevsky told the story of the time he was arrested by the Tsar and sentenced to die. The Tsar liked to play cruel psychological tricks on the people who rebelled against him, by blindfolding them and standing them in front of a firing squad. The blindfolded people would hear the gunshots go off, but would feel nothing. Then they would slowly realise that the guns were loaded with blanks.

Dostoevsky went through this experience himself. He said that going through the thought process of believing he was really going to die had a transforming effect on him. He talked about waking up that morning with full assurance that this would be his last day of life. He ate his last meal and savoured every bite. Every breath of air he took was precious to him. Every face he saw, he studied with full intensity. Suddenly, every experience was etched in his mind. As he was marched into the courtyard, he felt the heat of the sun and appreciated its warmth like never before. Everything around him seemed to have a magical quality to it. He was seeing the world in a way he had never seen it before. He was fully alive!

When Dostoevsky realised that he had not been shot and that he was not going to die that day, his life changed. He became thankful for everything.

He was even grateful to people he had previously despised. It was this experience that persuaded him to become a novelist and write about life in a way that before would have never been known to him. Dostoevsky was fully alive.

Keep Right with God

Finally, let's remember that however much we achieve on our journey in the world, it is our status with God that is of most importance. Consider Nicolaus Copernicus, a famed astronomer born in Poland on 19 February 1473. He was a mathematician whose accomplishments changed the world's ideas about the universe. He was also a well-known writer. Although highly educated in astronomical science, he was much more – he was a child of God who had learned to know and trust Jesus.

As he was lying critically ill, his book, *On the Resolutions of the Celestial Bodies*, which was hot off the press, was placed in his arms. But his thoughts were not of himself as an astronomer or scientist, but as a sinner who needed the forgiveness of his Saviour. He asked that the following epitaph be written on his gravestone: 'Lord, I do not ask the kindness Thou didst show to Peter. I do not dare ask the grace Thou didst grant to Paul; but, Lord, the mercy Thou didst show to the dying robber, that mercy show to me. That earnestly I pray.'

The Next Step

With courage and common sense, think about where and to whom God is directing you. Is your focus

> *With courage and common sense, think about where and to whom God is directing you.*

solely on him as you seek to take your first or next step? Are your thoughts on his glory or on your own fame and worldly success? Are you allowing your thoughts, words and deeds to be transformed as you become filled with the Holy Spirit? Are you willing to step out of your comfort zone in faith?

Keep on asking yourself these questions and seeking God for direction throughout your journey along the road to life. What one small step can you take towards God where you are and as you are, today?

Here is a final quote from the eighteenth century monk, Nicodemus of the Holy Mountain, which you might like to spend a moment reflecting on:

> You must know that progress on the path of spiritual life differs greatly from an ordinary journey on earth. If a traveller stops on his ordinary journey, he loses nothing of the way already covered; but if a traveller on the path of virtue stops in his spiritual progress, he loses much of the virtues previously acquired . . . In an ordinary journey, the further the traveller proceeds, the more tired he becomes, but on the way of spiritual life the longer a man travels . . . the greater the strength and power he acquires for his further progress.

Prayer

'Father God, I dedicate my future to you. I place it in your hands today. May you always keep me on the road to life, and would you lead me and guide me the whole way. I hand my worries about my next step over to you [tell God what these are now]. Equip me with both courage and discernment to know your voice and to obey it boldly. May my future bring you glory. Amen.'

Further Reading

Life Journeys: Stop Looking for the Will of God, Jeff Lucas, CWR, 2007 (This is a DVD resource with Bible notes.)
Life Journeys: A Walk on the Wild Side, Jeff Lucas, CWR, 2007 (This is a DVD resource with Bible notes.)
Glory Days: Living the whole of your life for Jesus, Julian Hardyman, Inter-Varsity Press, 2006
The Heart of Success, Rob Parsons, Hodder & Stoughton, 2002

11

Destination Heaven

Rihanna was a name that many people in the UK might not have been familiar with until the summer of 2007. The 19-year-old R&B singer's 'Umbrella' hit the top of our song charts and stayed there for a full ten weeks, becoming the longest running number one single since Whitney Houston's 'I Will Always Love You'. It was an impressive achievement.

But in an honest (and tearful) interview published in *The Sunday Times Culture* magazine, Rihanna said that despite achieving her dream, she felt unhappy. 'When you are in the spotlight, people are like, "What do you have to worry about?"' she says. 'They forget that the success is one great aspect of your life, but behind that there are problems, there are dark sides, there is loneliness, unhappiness.' Later in the interview, she talks about the time when while staying in Paris to promote her second album, she went out one day and had her long hair cut short. As soon as she returned home, 'someone in authority' made her put extensions back in her hair. Rihanna reveals the painful significance of this event, saying: 'It just crushed me . . . when you are 17, 18, that is when you are really trying to figure out who you are, and at that point I just wanted to try something out of the box. But as soon as you come out of your shell, like, "This is who I am", they just shove you back in with, "No, because this is what we want the box to look like." You just feel like a tool after a while.'

Reading Rihanna's raw words reminded me that our world's dream of fame is an empty one. Men and women have discovered time and again that once you get to the top, there is nothing there. Despite this, within human nature seems to be something that tells us to long for more in life, to strive, to struggle, to achieve. In her book *What You Always Wanted to Know about Heaven . . . But Were Afraid to Ask* (CWR, 2007), Catherine Butcher argues that this longing for perfection, completion or attainment within each one of us is in fact a yearning for heaven. She quotes the words in Ecclesiastes 3:11, 'He [God] has planted eternity in the human heart'. She then writes:

> *Within human nature seems to be something that tells us to long for more in life, to strive, to struggle, to achieve.*

> When the TV lottery show announces the winning combination, for a split second millions of people check their tickets and think: 'It could be me'. The flutter in their hearts might be heavily disguised, and laced with greed, but it is the hope of heaven – a better life hereafter.

It is the same when the divorced forty-something slips into a wedding dress and heads down the aisle for the second or third time. She is hoping for heaven – something more perfect, more intimate and more lasting.

When the ambitious young executive scans the job vacancies looking for the next career move, he is looking for heaven – satisfaction, fulfilment and the power to change futures . . .

The hope of heaven motivates millionaires and misers; house-proud homeowners and anxious asylum-seekers. Poets, artists and authors gain inspiration from it. Advertisers and marketing specialists make money because of it. It is the hope of heaven that gets us up in the morning. Though we might not recognise it, humanity's heart cry through the ages has always been: 'There must be more than this!'

> *The Bible teaches that there really is 'more than this' on offer for each and every one of us.*

The Bible teaches that there really is 'more than this' on offer for each and every one of us. In a sense, that is what this book has been all about. Jesus Christ offers us life with more purpose, meaning, satisfaction and healing than any other philosophy or way of living could ever give us.

Part of Christ's promise to his followers, whoever they are, is of a glorious future with him in heaven. Did you know that unique to the Christian faith is the concept of an afterlife that is not earned, but freely given by God? This chapter will take a closer look at what heaven is and the importance of living life with the knowledge that as Jesus' followers our final destination is heaven.

What Exactly is Heaven?

The Bible's teaching on heaven is full of wonderful paradoxes. In 1 Corinthians 2:9 we read: 'No eye has seen, no ear has heard, and no mind has imagined what God has prepared for those who love him.' Heaven is so amazing and incredulous that our tiny human minds cannot fully conceive it! But 1 Corinthians 2:10 says that the Holy Spirit does give us some understanding of what heaven is: 'It was to us that God revealed these things by his Spirit. For his Spirit searches out everything and shows us God's deep secrets.' Here are some further basics on heaven:

- In Genesis, we read that God created the heavens (Genesis 1:1). Heaven has existed since the beginning of time.
- God speaks, listens and sees all that happens on earth from his dwelling in heaven. Deuteronomy 26:15 says: 'Now look down from your holy dwelling place in heaven and bless your people Israel'.
- Psalm 78:23 says: 'But he commanded the skies to open; he opened the doors of heaven.' God is the only one in control of heaven – he decides who will and will not enter through its doors.
- The Psalms make reference to the 'armies of heaven'. These are likely to be the angels. 'Praise him, all his angels! Praise him, all the armies of heaven!' (Psalm 148:2).

The Kingdom of Heaven

A children's film came out before Christmas 2007 called *Mr Magorium's Wonder Emporium*, which explored the theme of death. In an interview about the film, its star Dustin Hoffman commented on how struck he was by the shocked reaction of many Americans to death being considered in a film for children. As we all know, birth and death are the only two events that every single one of us will face, no matter what. We are happy to talk about birth – but why in Western society are we so terrified to face death? As Christians we have no need to fear death, or to be silent on this important matter. Notably, Jesus' very first teachings focused on the kingdom of heaven, indicating that for him, the afterlife was hardly a topic to avoid discussing. In Matthew 4:17, we read: 'From then on Jesus began to preach, "Repent of your sins and turn to God, for the Kingdom of Heaven is near."' Jesus associated himself with the kingdom of heaven, indicating to his listeners both that he was divine, and that he was to bring heaven to earth through himself.

Here is what we learn about heaven through Jesus' teaching on the kingdom:

- Jesus said that the timing of the kingdom was past, present and future. God exists outside of time, therefore humans who lived before Jesus but who had had faith in God had already experienced the kingdom. Jesus brought the kingdom of heaven to his followers in the present through his own existence on earth. He would also bring in the kingdom in the future through his death on the cross, and later through the 'second coming', his future return to earth.

- Jesus showed his followers that a belief in heaven would start to change their thinking and behaviour in the present. 'Store your treasures in heaven, where moths and rust cannot destroy, and thieves do not break in and steal' (Matthew 6:20). Here Jesus was showing his disciples that material wealth and worldly achievement become less significant when you have a heavenly perspective on life. Instead, Jesus was saying, be someone who considers the things of God as treasure. These things will last into eternity.

- Jesus taught on who would enter into heaven, emphasising that God will make his judgement on the basis of who is a true disciple. 'Not everyone who calls out to me, "Lord! Lord!" will enter the Kingdom of Heaven. Only those who actually do the will of my Father in heaven will enter' (Matthew 7:21).

The Biggest Comeback of All Time

The Bible tells us that forty days after Jesus was resurrected from the dead, he ascended into heaven. It also tells us that he will come back to earth again a second time. Revelation 22:12,13 says: 'Look, I am coming soon, bringing my reward with me to repay all people according to their deeds. I am the Alpha and the Omega, the First and the Last, the Beginning and the End.'

> *The idea that Jesus will return in glory is not a minor or obscure belief of the lunatic fringe of Christianity.*

The idea that Jesus will return in glory is not a minor or obscure belief of the lunatic fringe of Christianity. In fact, it is to be found in more than 330 places in the New Testament and Jesus himself frequently talked about it. One whole book of the Bible, the book of Revelation, is based around the second coming of Jesus – this is not something that was added to the teaching of Jesus. The message of the second coming was always there and it cannot be removed from our Bibles without making a total nonsense of the text.

Jesus' return will be personal, visible and unmistakable. He will come in great power and glory. Unlike his last coming, it will not be done quietly; this time it will be no manger-and-stable job. When Jesus returns, it will not be an inconspicuous, unreported event. It will not merely be the end of our civilisation, but the end of our universe. No one living is going to overlook that! In fact, as the dead will be raised at the same time, even they won't miss it! Attendance at the second coming is going to be 100 per cent compulsory!

Let me give you a picture that may help explain the second coming. In the film *The Truman Show* Jim Carey plays Truman Burbank, a man who lives in a world that, unknown to him, is a total illusion.

It is merely a monstrously large stage set in which Truman is being constantly filmed for television. The plot revolves around Truman's dawning realisation that there is another world beyond his own, and his resulting escape from the studio set that has been his entire life.

The Bible indicates that in some ways we are like Truman: our world, too, is a theatre set. One day, though, instead of escaping out of it like Truman, God will suddenly take down the scenery and come in. As we see beyond the wreckage of all that we thought was reality, Jesus will stride out gloriously onto the set.

The Final Judgement

Jesus will finally judge the world at the second coming. For those who have, before death, repented of their sins and said 'yes' to Jesus there will be a welcome and they will go to be in joyful fellowship with him for ever. Jesus repeatedly spoke about how at this event, people would be divided into two groups: healthy crops and weeds (Matthew 13:24–30), fish that are edible and inedible (Matthew 13:47–52) and sheep and goats (Matthew 25:31–46). The divisions correspond to either eternal life or eternal death. This verdict, the Bible reiterates, is not going to

The only way of being sure that we will have God's approval and not his condemnation is to confess our sins and to believe and trust in Jesus.

be based on being a religious person, a regular churchgoer or even having done our best to live a good life. The only way of being sure that we will have God's approval and not his condemnation is to confess our sins and to believe and trust in Jesus.

The Resurrection of the Dead

In 1 Corinthians 15, Paul explains that at the second coming, the dead will be resurrected, just as Christ once was. Paul writes: 'Our earthly bodies are planted in the ground when we die, but they will be raised to live forever' (1 Corinthians 15:42). He continues to explain this phenomenon:

> Our bodies are buried in brokenness, but they will be raised in glory. They are buried in weakness, but they will be raised in strength. They are buried as natural human bodies, but they will be raised as spiritual bodies . . . What I am saying, dear brothers and sisters, is that our physical bodies cannot inherit the Kingdom of God. These dying bodies cannot inherit what will last forever.
>
> But let me reveal to you a wonderful secret. We will not all die, but we will all be transformed! It will happen in a moment, in the blink of an eye, when the last trumpet is blown. For when the trumpet sounds, those who have died will be raised to live forever. And we who are living will also be transformed. For our dying bodies must be transformed into bodies that will never die; our mortal bodies must be transformed into immortal bodies.
> (1 Corinthians 15:43–44,50–53)

Let's allow the truth that one day we will each be given a heavenly, immortal body to challenge our sometimes perfectionist attitudes towards our bodies in the present.

When Will All This Happen?

Jesus said very plainly that the date and time of his return were unknown and would remain so until the event happened. That has not stopped some people trying to guess the year and month – so far with a spectacularly consistent failure rate! Christ's coming again might occur before you have read the end of this book, but equally, it might not come for another 10,000 years! On Jesus' return all evil will abruptly and finally be ended; the great rebellion will at last be over.

How Should We Respond to the Second Coming?

As Jesus' followers we are not to try and pin down the date of the second coming. Christ was ambiguous about when he would return, perhaps so that we would continue to follow him with passion rather than ticking off the days left! Let's remember that when Jesus returns, it will be too late for those who have chosen to reject him to swap to his side. Their decision will have already been permanently made. This urges us on to reach others with his message before it is too late!

At the same time we are to remain assured that Jesus will, on his return, sweep his followers up into heaven with

> *Let's remember that when Jesus returns, it will be too late for those who have chosen to reject him to swap to his side.*

him. We must live in celebration of the incredible things to come in heaven for us as God's people. John 14:1–3 says:

> 'Don't let your hearts be troubled. Trust in God, and trust also in me. There is more than enough room in my Father's home. If this were not so, would I have told you that I am going to prepare a place for you? When everything is ready, I will come and get you, so that you will always be with me where I am.'

What Will Heaven be Like?

Jesus said that after the final judgement, the whole world will be transformed – a new heaven and a new earth will be made. Here is what this wonderful place will be like:

- Both the Old Testament and the New Testament emphasise the glorious, restorative perfection of heaven. The Bible's picture is of a place of abundance, feasting, dancing and enjoyment. Heaven is described as a luscious garden – the image is of the Garden of Eden in its restored state. Another biblical image for heaven is of a royal wedding; the picture is of Christ being perfectly united with his bride, the church.
- The image that Jesus used most to describe heaven was of a banquet – I see no reason why we should not call it a party! Revelation 19:17 says: 'Then I saw an angel standing in the sun, shouting to the vultures flying high in the sky: "Come! Gather together for the great banquet God has prepared."'

- Heaven is described as a place of victory; the power, goodness and love of God will finally overcome evil and sin in our world. If hell is the place where nothing good can exist, heaven is the place where nothing bad can survive. Heaven will be a time of healing, restoration and freedom.
- Revelation 21:1–4 describes heaven as the New Jerusalem: 'Then I saw a new heaven and a new earth, for the old heaven and the old earth had disappeared. And the sea was also gone. And I saw the holy city, the new Jerusalem, coming down from God out of heaven like a bride beautifully dressed for her husband.

   I heard a loud shout from the throne, saying, "Look, God's home is now among his people! He will live with them, and they will be his people. God himself will be with them. He will wipe every tear from their eyes, and there will be no more death or sorrow or crying or pain. All these things are gone forever."'
- Not only will heaven have a wonderful quality about it; there will also be a wonderful quantity about it! Quite simply, unlike every other wonderful time we have ever experienced, heaven will go on forever.

Hope in Death

Sheryl Crow once said: 'The beauty of having a producer is that you have someone who says: you are finished.' She was talking about a music producer of course – but her words can be applied to the outlook of the Christian, too. There is incredible freedom in knowing that God our maker is in control of our lives, our destinies and the time of our departure from this earth.

In her book *Destiny's Children* (Kingsway Publications), Anita Cleverly tells the tragic story of a baby born to loving Christian parents with a heart not properly formed. After having had extensive surgery and looking as though she might begin to recover, tiny Jessica died at just a few months old. Reflecting on this short life, Anita writes:

> A question has lingered with me since that day; did Jessica fulfil more of a destiny in three short months than many a mortal who walks the earth for three score years and ten? If it is true that before you were formed in the womb God knew you; you were set apart; that all the days ordained for you were written in your book; several thoughts follow . . . the quality of our life is more significant than the quantity . . . [and] finding out what God set us apart for is of much greater importance than securing a well-ordered life and bank balance.

Anita goes on to remind her readers that Jesus 'supremely fulfilled his destiny' during his short life of just 33 years.

> *Jesus 'supremely fulfilled his destiny' during his short life of just 33 years.*

You Are a Citizen of Heaven

It is in honestly facing death that Paul reveals the incredible depth of his own sense of life purpose. He writes: 'I trust that my life will bring honour to Christ, whether I live or die. For to me, living means living for Christ, and dying is even better. But if I live, I can do more fruitful work for Christ' (Philippians 1:20,21). For Paul, death represents hope, future glory and resurrection life. Later in this chapter of Philippians, Paul challenges the church to live as citizens of heaven in the present. If you have begun a relationship with Jesus, you are a citizen of heaven. Are you thinking and living like one?

Your Response to Jesus

What is Christianity? In essence it is an invitation from King Jesus to you and me – offering us forgiveness for the past, re-birth into new life in the present and a real hope for an eternal future. If we are not in relationship with God our creator and king, life can seem purposeless. Bob Dylan once said: 'I change during the course of a day. I wake and I'm one person, and when I go to sleep I know for certain I'm somebody else.' Jesus offers you a secure identity as his child, and a life full of meaning.

RSVP. Reply, please. What have you done with your invitation while you have been reading this book? If you haven't accepted your invitation yet, you can accept it now. If you are not sure whether or not you have really accepted it, now would be a good time to accept it properly.

Making a real response to Jesus is essential – if you don't, you are simply keeping all that you have read in this book as theory, when it needs to be put into practice! It is a bit like going to a GP and saying, 'I've got this rash, can you help?' You leave with a prescription from the doctor.

When you walk out of the surgery, have you got the answer? Well you have and you haven't. You have to go to the pharmacy, get the cream and you have to apply it. Many people get the diagnosis and get the prescription but they don't apply it. You now know a lot about God, but are you really applying what you have discovered? You may have once embarked on a spiritual journey, perhaps long ago, but have since strayed from God. If you are not yet using the treatment that he offers you, ask him for healing and empowerment to become the person you are meant to be.

Ask now. If you haven't made a commitment to Jesus yet, I suggest you pray this prayer:

Jesus Christ, I open the door of my life to you now. Come in by your Holy Spirit. Fill me with your presence and your peace. Help me to validate my faith in you in thought, word and deed. Thank you for hearing my prayer. Amen.

The New You

> *Being a Christian means living a new life.*

Being a Christian means living a new life – we die to our old lives and begin a new one, with a completely refreshed heart. Knowing who we have become by accepting Christ enables us to travel this road. Paul writes of his new life with

Jesus: 'My old self has been crucified with Christ. It is no longer I who live, but Christ lives in me. So I live in this earthly body by trusting in the Son of God, who loved me and gave himself for me' (Galatians 2:20).

My prayer for you is that whatever comes your way; you would cling on to the immense power of our God, and continue in the new life that you have been called to. In Isaiah 40:31 we read, ' . . . those who trust in the LORD will find new strength. They will soar high on wings like eagles. They will run and not grow weary. They will walk and not faint.' In recent weeks I have become fascinated and intrigued by this incredible bird. The eagle makes its nest from briars and thorns and then lines the nest with animal skin, to stop the thorns and briars hurting the newly hatched eaglets. Mum brings the food, and the eaglets hang around the nest getting fat. Until one day, when Mum decides it is time to fly . . .

Naturally, the eaglets are not keen. The mother eagle gently pulls away the animal skins and eventually the eaglets are eager to leave the nest. They clamber on their mother's back and she flies high, reaching around 5000 ft over the ground. This is not the time for the eaglets to suffer from vertigo! Suddenly, the mother tips the eaglet off and it goes hurtling down. It flaps its wings but nothing happens. The earth looks closer and closer. Just as the eaglet is about to be splattered all over the ground, the mother eagle swoops down and catches the eaglet and the process is repeated until the eaglet learns to fly.

And so it is with us in the Christian life. When we first become Christians we feel protected in the nest, but God soon takes us out of it, so that he can teach us to 'soar on wings like eagles'. We need to continue to have faith that God will come down and rescue us when we can't quite manage to do what he requires of us. If we want to soar, we need to learn to trust in God. Remember what Jesus said: 'Don't let your hearts be troubled. Trust in God, and trust also in me' (John 14:1). Proverbs 3:5,6 (NIV) says: 'Trust in the LORD with all your heart and lean not on your own understanding; in all your ways acknowledge him, and he will make your paths straight.'

Press On

The athlete Kelly Holmes received many, many setbacks during her injury-prone career, and at several points she was tempted to give it all up and retire. Hers was a story of perseverance, struggle, dogged determination and dedication – and in the end, triumph. She eventually won two gold medals at the Olympics in Athens in 2004. Two thousand years ago, Paul wrote to the Philippian Christians: 'One thing I do: Forgetting what is behind and straining towards what is ahead, I press on towards the goal to win the prize for which God has called me heavenwards in Christ Jesus' (Philippians 3:13,14, NIV).

Eternal life is to live the life that God lives – WOW! That is

> *Eternal life is to live the life that God lives – WOW!*

quite a thought, to 'live the life that God lives'. Let's live our lives here on earth in the light of eternity and let God live in us and work through us so that we reflect the attributes of being a 'citizen of heaven'. This is the purpose that God has for you; it is your soul purpose. Enjoy it! As the ancient Latin blessing for a journey states, 'Deus vobiscum': may God go with you.

Prayer

In the words written in the Bible's penultimate verse:

'Amen! Come, Lord Jesus!'

Further Reading

What You Always Wanted to Know about Heaven . . . But Were Afraid to Ask, Catherine Butcher, CWR, 2007
26 Steps to Heaven, J.John, Hodder & Stoughton, 2007
Sign up for J.John's free motivational weekly email letter: www.philotrust.com

Appendix A

Selecting a Bible

Finding a Bible in a version that resonates with you will help you engage with the Word of God. Here are some suggestions to assist you in this:

- *Life Application Study Bible*, published by Tyndale House. This Bible is the New Living Translation, a modern version that stays very close to the original languages. Bible quotations in *Soul Purpose* are taken from the New Living Translation.
- *Franklin NIV 450*. This is an electronic device containing the New International Version of the Bible, which is a slightly more conservative translation, but also very true to biblical scholarship. As a portable, electronic Bible, this device has excellent search functions, so you can quickly and easily access passages that you are interested in, or do keyword searches.
- If you want a paper version of the same translation, try the *NIV Life Application Study Bible*, published by Kingsway.

- *The Message*, Eugene Peterson, published by Navpress. This version of the Bible is written in contemporary language.
- Navpress also publish *The Message // REMIX*, a version of *The Message* written especially for young people. It includes a commentary, lessons and devotional questions.
- *New Century Version Youth Bible*, published by Authentic Media. This youth Bible includes the 'Life Files' (more than 470 real life stories relating the Bible to young people today) background facts, more than 50 maps and diagrams, a dictionary and topical concordance.
- *New American Standard Version* (wide margin reference edition), published by Cambridge University. This format allows space to scribble in your thoughts and questions as you read. I also find this a very readable translation.
- *Daily Study Bible for Women*, published by Tyndale House.
- *Daily Study Bible for Men*, published by Tyndale House.
- *Cover to Cover Complete*, published by CWR. This is the Bible ordered chronologically. It includes Bible notes, timelines, maps and illustrations.
- www.biblegateway.com is a fantastic online Bible search engine.

Appendix B

Selecting Daily Bible Reading Notes

Daily Bible notes that bring the Word of God to life are essential to my Bible reading. Try a few different ones to see which you enjoy. Here are my suggestions:

- A free and very readable guide is *The Word For Today*, published by United Christian Broadcasters. Each booklet contains suggested readings with commentary for every day over a 3 month period. Copies can be requested by email (ucb@ucb.co.uk) or by phone (0845 60 40 401). See www.ucb.co.uk
- UCB also publish a version of *The Word For Today* for young people called *The World 4U 2Day*. See www.ucb.co.uk
- *Every Day With Jesus for New Christians*, Selwyn Hughes, published by CWR. These accessible notes will help you get to grips with all the basics of the Christian life.
- CWR also publish Bible notes written by Jeff Lucas – *Lucas on Life Every Day*.

- *30 Days*, Nicky Gumbel, published by Alpha International. If you are beginning to explore the Bible, these 30 short Bible readings (designed to be read over 30 days) would make a great introduction.
- The Soul Survivor online magazine has a Bible study section: see www.soulsurvivor.com/magazine
- *Closer to God* in print and online at www. closertogod.org.uk/ is for anyone wanting to read the Bible in the power of the Holy Spirit.